882

12⁵⁰

THE BOOK OF FURNITURE
AND DECORATION:

PERIOD AND MODERN

The Book of Furniture and Decoration:

PERIOD AND MODERN

by

JOSEPH ARONSON

CROWN PUBLISHERS

NEW YORK

COPYRIGHT, 1936, 1941, BY
CROWN PUBLISHERS

Revised, February, 1941

ENGRAVINGS BY CHEMICAL ENGRAVING CO.
PRINTED AND BOUND BY THE HADDON CRAFTSMEN, SCRANTON, PA.

CONTENTS

PART I

THE DEVELOPMENT OF DECORATION

CHAPTER		PAGE
I	Introductory	15
II	Italy	22
	Italian Gothic	22
	Italian Renaissance	23
	Baroque	25
III	Spain	27
	Spanish Renaissance	27
IV	France	31
	French Renaissance	32
	Provincial French	65
	Louis XIII	66
	The Regal Age of Louis XIV	68
	Regence	74
V	France: After Louis XIV	76
	The Feminine Furniture of Louis XV	76
	The Classic Revival Under Louis XVI	81
	The Antique Empire Style	84
VI	England	90
	The Age of Oak: Gothic and Renaissance	90
	Tudor and Elizabethan	92
	Jacobean	95
VII	England: The Age of Walnut	131
	William and Mary	131
	Queen Anne	134
VIII	England: The Age of Mahagony	137
	Early Georgian	137
	Chippendale	140

v

CHAPTER   PAGE

IX   England: The Age of Satinwood 145
       The Adam Brothers 145
       Hepplewhite 147
       Sheraton 149
       Other Georgian Designers and Craftsmen . . . 151

 X   The Nineteenth Century 152
       England: The Regency 152
       Victoria 153
       Germany 155

XI   Early American 157
       New England 159
       New York and the Dutch 161
       The South 162

XII The Federal Period and After 165
       American Empire and Later American Styles . . 166

XIII The Twentieth Century 171

XIV Contemporary Design 174

PART II

THE ELEMENTS OF DECORATION

XV   Materials of Decoration 189
       Furniture Woods 191
       Frequently Used Woods 228
       Imported Woods 233
       Less Frequently Used Woods 234
       Wood Finishes 240
       Willow, Wicker and Fibre 241
       Metals in Furniture 242
       Glass in Furniture 245
       Plastics 246

XVI Fabrics 249
       Unfigured Fabrics 251
       Leather 253

XVII Wall Coverings 255
       Ceilings 258

XVIII Floor Coverings 259

CONTENTS

CHAPTER   PAGE

XIX   Decorative Objects 263

           Pictures 265

           Sculpture 267

           Musical Instruments 270

           Screens 272

           Living Plants 273

XX   Color 275

           The Planning of Color Schemes 279

           Mixing Paints 283

XXI   Lighting 285

           Architectural Lighting 289

XXII   Windows and Window Treatment 291

XXIII   Furniture and How to Buy It 297

PART III

THE PRINCIPLES OF DECORATION

XXIV   Room Planning and Arrangement 311

           The Architecture of the Room 311

           The Plan 313

XXV   Rooms 317

           Foyer or Entry-Hall 318

           Function of Living Rooms 318

           The Formal Living Room or Drawing Room . . 320

           Living Room 330

           Bedroom 333

           Combination Rooms 337

           Dining Room 340

           Library 342

           Guest Rooms 342

           Nursery 343

           Child's Room 344

           Miscellaneous Rooms 345

XXVI   Seasonal Changes 348

Bibliography 350

Index 353

ILLUSTRATIONS

ALL LINE DRAWINGS BY THE AUTHOR

PAGE

16th Cent. English Dining Room. *French and Co.* 33
Early Italian Interior 35
Decorated Ceiling of the Middle Renaissance 36
Living Room of the Italian Renaissance.
                     Mary Coggeshall-Jeanette Jukes, Dec. 36
Old Italian Rooms 37
Italian Baroque Rooms 38
Italian Rococo Rooms 39
Spanish Furniture 40, 41
Spanish Renaissance Interiors 42
Room With French Gothic Furniture 43
Gothic Furniture With Architectural Background 44
Library in the Style of Louis XVI 45
Bedroom in the Style of Louis XVI 45
Late 18th Cent. French Furniture. *Nancy McClelland, Dec.* . 46
Bedroom, Chateau de Mereville. *Sarah Hunter Kelly, Dec.* . 46
Wall Painting, Style of Louis XVI. *Ruth C. Bigelow, Dec.* . 47
Louis XV Furniture 48
Louis XVI Furniture 49
Bedroom Walls Covered With Toile de Jouy. *Hubert Robert, Dec.* 50
French Furniture, Directoire Style 51
Directoire Wall Paper 52
Directoire Toiles de Jouy 52
Napoleon's Desk 52
Empire Secretaire 52
Bedroom in Directoire Style 53
Room in English Gothic Style 54
English Linenfold Panelling 55
Jacobean Furniture 55
English Furniture of Various Periods 56
Oriental Rugs and Tapestries With English Furniture 57
English Furniture of the 18th Century 58, 59
Early Georgian Pine Woodwork 60
18th Century Pine Panelled Room 61
English Panelling in a Modern Apartment. *Ida Webster, Arch.* . 61
Chippendale, Hepplewhite, and Sheraton Pieces 62
Georgian Furniture and Woodwork 63

ix

PAGE

Regency Furniture 63
Chippendale and Sheraton Furniture 64
Pilgrim Furniture 97
New England Interior 97
Chinese Ornaments 98, 99
New Hampshire Farmhouse 100
Bedroom, Springfield, Mass., 1754 100
Painted Panels, Dutch Influence 101
18th Cent. Bedroom, Surry County, Virginia 101
Chinese Wallpaper, Philadelphia, 1768 101
Pennsylvania German Decoration 102
Hasbrouck House, Ulster County, N. Y. 102
Scenic Wallpaper, Virginia, 1760 103
Painted Wood Panelling, Virginia, 1750 103
Bedroom in Homewood, Baltimore County, Maryland, c. 1799 . 104
Bedroom, Alexandria, Virginia, c. 1752 104
Early 19th Century American Decoration 105
Late 18th Century American Furniture 106
American Empire Room 106
Music Room, 1800 107
American Interpretations of Hepplewhite and Sheraton . . . 107
Early 19th Century Furniture. *Katherine Park Studdiford, Dec.* . 108
Chairs and Sofa of the Federal Period. *Ruth C. Bigelow, Dec.* . 108
The 19th Century in America 109
House of William Lescaze, Architect 110
Modern Interior. *Eugene Schoen, Architect* 111
Classic Designs Freely Interpreted 112, 113
House of Morris B. Sanders, Architect 114
Contrasting Patterns and Textures 115
Living Room by William Muschenheim 116
Corner Treatments 117
Dining Room. *C. Coggeshall, Designer* 118
Open Plan House. *Joseph Allen Stein, Architect* 119
Living Rooms 120
California Living Room. *Richard Neutra, Architect* 121
Dining Room. *John Funk, Architect* 121
Rooms Designed by Robert Heller 122
Pine Panelling, With Bookcases. *Roy Barley, Decorator* . . . 123
Walls of Wood 124
Living Room. *Joseph Mullen, Designer* 125
Colliers' House of Ideas. *E. Stone, Arch., D. Cooper, Dec.* . . 125
Decorative Wallpapers 126
Scenic Wallpapers 127
Strong Architectural Features. *Margery Sill Wickware, Dec.* . 128
Painted Overdoor. *Edna Kern, Decorator* 128
Classic Derivations in Modern Design. *Robsjohn-Gibbings, Dec.* 193
Wood Floor in a French Chateau. *Sarah Hunter Kelly, Dec.* . 194

ILLUSTRATIONS

PAGE

House of Almos Evans, Architect 195
Screen Panel of Ribbed Glass. *Joseph Aronson, Designer* . . . 196
Vista Through a Doorway. *Harrie T. Lindeberg, Arch.* . . . 197
Rugs 198
Decorative Treatment of Stairway. *Alexander H. Girard, Arch.* . 199
Discipline in Decorative Objects. *S. U. and M., Decorators* . 200
Dressing Table Group. *Margery Sill Wickware, Decorator* . 201
Important Sculpture on Adequate Base. *A. H. Girard, Arch.* . 202
Decorative Use of Leather 203
Architectural Lighting 204
Concealed Lighting. *Morris B. Sanders, Architect* 205
Brilliant Crystal Lighting Fixture 206
Vertical Indirect Illumination. *William Lescaze, Arch.* . . . 207
Ingenuity in Lighting 208
Dressing Room. *Smyth, Urquhart and Marckwald, Decorators* . 209
Architectural Lighting. *Virginia Connor, Designer* 210
Dining Room. *James F. Eppenstein, Designer* 211
Window Treatments 212
Dining Room. *Miss Gheen, Decorator* 212
Foyer. *Paul MacAlister, Designer* 213
Classic Doorway. *Salomonsky, Arch., Schlimme, Dec.* . . . 214
Living Room. *Harwell Hamilton Harris, Architect* 215
Ingenious Use of Small Space 216
Decoration Subordinated to Architectural Forms 217
Scale and Balance in Design. *Robsjohn-Gibbings, Designer* . . 218
Rooms With a View 219
Rooms Designed by Paul Laszlo 220
Rooms Designed by Paul MacAlister 221
Bedroom. *Harold Schwartz, Designer* 222
Living Room. *C. Coggeshall, Designer* 223
Combination Rooms. *Joseph Aronson, Designer* 224
18th Century Dining Room. *Virginia* 321
New England Pine Cupboard 321
Modern Dining Rooms 322
Dining Room. *Robsjohn-Gibbings, Designer* 323
Balance Through Symmetry. *Margery Sill Wickware, Decorator* 324
Room For a Small Boy. *Joseph Aronson, Designer* 325
Nursery, and Juvenile Furniture. *Ilonka Karasz, Designer* . 326
Parents' Retreat. *William Muschenheim, Architect* 327
Living Room. *Eugene Schoen, Architect* 328

THE BOOK OF FURNITURE AND
DECORATION

PART I

THE DEVELOPMENT OF DECORATION

CHAPTER I

INTRODUCTORY

The need for shelter was one of the first urges felt by Man. When he began to do something about it he was guided to a great extent by what we now recognize as the sense of beauty. Primitive though his covering, cave or cliff-dwelling might have been, its success in pleasing the eye of himself, his woman or children was noted. Whether it was an ornament, a drawing or a method of arrangement, if he liked it he used it. And what is more, preferences were developed and passed on to future generations.

Since beauty is essentially a personal affair, there never were, nor can there ever be, specific definitions of what is beautiful. There are undoubtedly a great many points about which most people have been in agreement. At certain times opinions have swung from one attitude to another. However, the effect of applying a number of these ideas to decoration at a particular time has led to the development of styles or periods.

Architecture is the art or science of building. Materials, ideas, and human abilities contribute to producing the complete structure. The design and process of erecting the exterior should not be isolated from the decoration of the inside. Both join to prepare the building for its complete function. The decoration of the interior depends upon similar principles and has developed from the same urges.

15

Primitive man probably did his first embellishment of the inside of the cave himself. It is idle to speculate as to just when this function was delegated to the woman of the household.

The breadwinner went forth and left the women at home, to embroider and prettify and rearrange the furniture; so that when women came out boldly and asserted themselves, they spoke most emphatically of their special domain: the house. The architects, who considered themselves really equipped for the task of decoration by reason of their training and background, remained aloof. Hence the cleavage in the first third of this century between the fields of the architect and the interior decorator.

During the past few years, however, these two have begun to collaborate once more; but collaboration is not enough. Unity is the basis of fine design. The architect cannot say to the engineer: "Build your building, and I will dress it up." Neither can he say to the interior decorator: "Here is a house—dress it up." The architect is the fundamental planner from beginning to end. He must see the whole picture, not of a cold empty house, but one warm with activity, with people moving busily and cheerfully and happily in their appropriate background.

The separate job of the interior decorator is to recognize the primary importance of the dwelling itself. This is not a matter of style. It is rather the understanding of the nature of the room and the material available. That is to say: This is a living room. It has these natural physical characteristics. It will therefore perform its stated functions within the restrictions of these charac-

PREHISTORIC

PRIMITIVE VIEAVING.

teristics. This will make it look so and so. Thus, we provide for utility, and organize its appearance.

It remains then to choose the manner and the materials. Shall it be gay? or restful? or studious? or frivolous? or monastic? This is the individual element. Let us not ask, "Shall it be Louis XVI? or modern? or Turkish Cozy Corner?" Rather ask what or whom we want to express, and how to express it.

Historically, certain large moods have enveloped whole peoples at given times. Their era, or period, acquires definite distinctive characteristics. The time and the place produce a style. Ever afterward, these people are known by the poems they wrote, the ideas they expounded, the chairs they sat upon. The air of a 16th century Italian Palazzo is distinct from that of a 1750 New England farmhouse, because the people who created the one house were entirely different from the people who created the other.

We do not in this book propose that you adopt either as a background. Our purpose is to show how the various moods grew and took form in rooms and furniture; the living technique behind the forms and how they may be serviceable to us today.

The fashion of looking backward for style has always existed. Sometimes we look further back for inspiration than at other times. The extent of this depends on the current mood and conditions. If we find, among the relics of bygone age, certain ideas that are like our immediate demands, we adopt or adapt them. There is no harm in this; all true artistic growth has been along evolutionary lines. But in depending upon the past we are likely to fall into an erroneous line of development.

The danger lies in the fact that, gaining enthusiasm for these relics, we may begin to live for them, to re-create a background for them instead of using them as best we may in a background for ourselves. If we distort all the fine achievements of our own time, in order to accommodate those relics, we abuse the beauty of the antiques; we are guilty of aesthetic deceit, of stage setting. If we misuse new materials in order to achieve a sham resemblance to old things, we do not profit by other growths, we merely imitate them, and imitation is the death of art.

No historical style set itself out to be what it became, either as to form or name. There was always a steady change of feeling, a craving for something new. The builder was always free to use everything he knew. This material whether out of the past or present was his source of inspiration. What he did to it was his interpretation. This is what will invariably happen. The rudest construction of a table interprets the maker's taste in choice of material, size, proportion. If he sees other tables, he borrows features that he likes. The interpretation is more distinctive than the inspiration; it becomes in fact his own style. The influences and effects, the impact of new materials, the special exigencies of the time and place, are all factors. The following outline of the growth of the art of interior decoration is concerned primarily with the way the factors worked and what they produced.

Certain similarities existed in different times and places. These produced furniture of such harmonious types that they may be combined with satisfactory results, as we shall indicate.

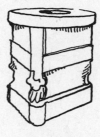

Customarily books on furniture or interior decorating begin at the beginning, work down thru the Flood, Cro-Magnon man, Egypt, Greece and the Grandeur that was Rome. This very thorough procedure is fascinating and instructive, but generally of small aid to the general reader. Since we are concerned with historical architecture chiefly for inspiration and comparison, we will spend little time on the beginnings of decoration. We will start our historical inquiry at the point at which rooms began to assume a form faintly comparable to that of today . . . specialized, deliberate, purposeful.

ASSYRIAN
ALTAR

Actually, the same forces operate about the same time; it is astonishing to what degree influences in style travelled about Europe and Asia at a time when most nations held themselves almost incommunicado. The differences in exact time and place cause the interpretations to vary, but the same impulse breaks out like a rash, first here, then there.

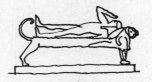

There have been in the past thousand years a few positively defined movements, based on great developments in the conception of man and his surroundings. To the generations to whom this occurred it was the change from the old fashioned to the new; but the perspective of a few hundred years permits us a different analysis. For the purposes of this book we have five of these major distinctions, each a reaction from the previous one.

· EGYPTIAN ·

THE GOTHIC, an epoch of church dominance.

THE RENAISSANCE, period of political growth.

BAROQUE OR ROCOCO, CLASSIC REVIVAL { Both appendages of the Renaissance but at odds as to its objective.

MODERN, the epoch of industrial domination which began with the Industrial Revolution.

It is least confusing to follow this development in a restricted locale, so we shall isolate Italy and Spain, France, England, and America, and consider them as sequential. In each of these lands to a greater or lesser degree we may observe the approach and decline of each major phase. About 1400, the beginning of the Renaissance, none of these countries existed as we know them, but the move to nationalization was beginning— and with it the development of specialized characteristics. These are not the only sources of decorating history, but for our study, they are most logically in line and include most of the features of interest.

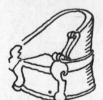

The early history of decoration and furniture is interesting chiefly as a source of motifs, or the way in which it influenced later, more applicable styles. From prehistoric times we have some few elements of decorative design—the symbols that were painted or woven or scratched into rock. In Egypt, Babylonia, Assyria, and Persia, grew the arts that used and adapted these themes. Greece and Rome developed and invented an untold variety of decoration motifs. But their actual furniture, their actual rooms give us nothing, except as seen through the eyes of later periods.

After the evaporation of the Roman Empire came a

GREEK

thousand years of confusion. In Southern Europe classic and Oriental themes gave birth to the Byzantine, a Mediterranean brilliance of gold and mosaic. Saracenic influence via Spain brought in the Oriental strain which spread as far as Scandinavia, but left in Spain and Northern Africa an ineradicable quality.

The classic Roman solidified and simplified into primitive Romanesque; in which form it spread north through the peoples that later settled down to being French and German and English. Upon the crude classicism left by the Roman conquerors, the various wild tribes imposed forms of materialistic and symbolic ornament.

By the year 1100, we have a clear and unique style, the Gothic. This was purely architectural in expression. It grew out of a great wave of religious fervor. Naturally the church was the highest expression of the art; secular life was subordinated, and the domestic was the least of that. The style was so spontaneous that it developed a high degree of individuality in each country, although all possessed a similar series of religious symbols. The various geographical Gothics rose and gave way to the Renaissance, early in some places, later in others, but in every case the transition from Gothic to Renaissance marks the commencement of interior architecture as we know it. It is the beginning of modern times.

ROMAN

CHAPTER II

ITALY

ITALIAN GOTHIC

IRON WORK

CHEST.

ITALIAN GOTHIC.

Old John Evelyn, eighty-two years old, who had retired from his last minor position to live in the house at Wotton that had been his brother's, wrote rather peevishly in his diary, in 1702, of faultless classic buildings, "They were demolished by the Goths or Vandals, who introduced their own licentious style now called modern or Gothic." This flowering of the Middle Ages in pointed arches of stone that climbed upward toward the clouds appeared first in France about 1100 and spread southward to Italy. It is doubtful if it derived from the Goths, of whose buildings not even a description remains. It grew from the vaulted forests of northern Europe, and Italy was not as rich in these as more northerly countries. Italian Gothic never took kindly to the pointed arch; it leaned more toward color, as in the Byzantine flamboyance of St. Mark's Cathedral in Venice, or the flawless beauty of Giotto's campanile at Florence. There never was a true Gothic style in Italy; there was no need for it. The brilliant climate demanded cool dim interiors; small windows in thick walls, rather than the vast traceried windows of French Gothic. The climate, plus the survival of a classic breadth of conception, led to spacious interiors with great wall surfaces on which the fresco painters and mosaic makers could work to their heart's content. There was a certain security and splendor about medieval life in the northern Italian cities; Florence, Venice, Pisa, Siena and Bologna were rich in palaces that were gay and elegant beyond anything in contemporary Europe. The actual furnishings were sparse, but the specialized room became a fact.

ITALIAN RENAISSANCE

During the 14th century one of those extraordinary explosions of thought occurred in Italy. It ultimately touched everything, everywhere. It spread like the ripples made by a stone cast into quiet water. The Italians call it Rinascimenta: we know it better by the French Renaissance. It was the new birth of the spirit of inquiry: a new social life prevailed: art, commerce, letters, science,—every human activity broke its fetters.

Life became brighter, gayer, more open. The rooms in which these activities took place blossomed out. An outburst of decorative enthusiasm fostered the creation of new furniture ideas. The fact that the Italians respected classic Rome as the ultimate in achievement made them cherish the classic motifs of Rome and Greece. They evaluated and formulated classic architecture, and their decorative forms were chiefly miniature architecture.

Araberque.

The earliest Italian Renaissance rooms were simple of wall, with high raftered ceilings. The earlier stone walls were hung with tapestries; about the 13th century a form of tiling called Cosmatic mosaic was introduced. Later the discovery of the stuccoes of ancient Rome inspired the mural painters. Raphael and his school

CARYATID

covered acres of walls with friezes, panels and ara-
besques; by 1500 the richness of wall treatment reached
its highest point. Wainscoting and rich tapestries,
leathers, gold and silk fabrics as well as painting made
rich backgrounds. Squares of marbleized paper called
Domino were used as wall decoration after 1500. The
ceilings were developed correspondingly. Intense colors and gold shone out of the subdued, warm light.

The furniture that graced these rooms was, at first,
simple and rigid in outline and extremely sparse. The
great hall had a dominant table, a few stiff rectangular
chairs and cassone (chests) and credenza (cabinets).
Conditions were still unsettled enough to make these
portable elements necessary; in a pinch the valuables
could be carried away in them. They served as seats and
storehouses. Oak and walnut were the dominant woods;
gilding and polychrome were increasingly used. High
color was employed everywhere; the lovely softening
patina of these old colors is a product of time, not in-
tent. Ivory and metal and the typical tarsia (inlay), a
Byzantine bequest, appeared everywhere. Classic carving grew to cover everything—masks, gargoyles, birds,
caryatids, animals, trophies, centaurs,—all combined
with free scrolls and yielded a fine animation against
the remote background. Marble tops for cabinets and
consoles are identified with the 16th century.

Weaving had always been high in Italian achievements; silk was woven in many towns after the year
1000. Persian patterns were copies, and about 1300
Genoa began to design silks and velvets in the Eastern
manner. Italian weavers carried the technique of silk
and velvet all over Europe but Flemish workmen came

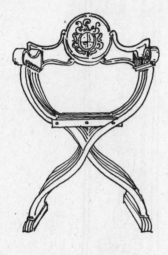

SAVONAROLA CHAIR

CRADLE

to Italy to weave the wool tapestries designed by Italians after 1400. The splendid velvets came after 1500, which was the richest period in Italian weaving; it saw the development of the magnificent damasks of Venice and Lucca.

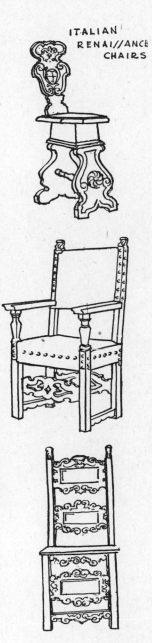

ITALIAN
RENAISSANCE
CHAIRS

BAROQUE

Up to 1650 the general aspect of Italian furniture was one of highly enriched restraint. After that time they dropped the restraint. Room architecture erupted into broken pediments, huge scrolls, ill-applied sculpture, a general exaggeration of scale and line and color. The fine sense of fitness of objects gave way completely to the theatrical, the obvious, the purely decorative, a ponderous wedding cake decoration. Brilliant color schemes, marble floors, exciting, riotous shapes expressed a restlessness, corruption, empty wealth. But these were not longer the great Medicis, Sforzas, Farnese, Estes, Borgias; the little ones of those names were ghosts of their former greatness. Their artists were too self-conscious, too sophisticated and exhibited the swing from aesthetic action to reaction. Seventeenth and eighteenth century Italian decoration is elegant to a fault, theatrical, finicky, overdecorated, structurally weak and architecturally thin; its soul was that of a painted withered old marchese. Italy's contribution to the 18th century flare of classicism was a light, decorative, utterly charming style which was thoroughly cloying. Delicate color schemes of white, ivory and grey with gold; painted walls cleverly decorated, marble-inlaid floors, or floors of matched woods; the entire picture lightly colorful, bright, brittle.

It is important to remember that at no time did any of this decorative art represent any section of society other than the ruling caste. Nobody else had furniture worth the name, let alone style. What the poor, the artisans, the great mass, used was probably of the simplest, and cheapest; but we do not know. The Italian Renaissance style is one of nobility, the grand manner. It expresses admirably a bold, exuberant scale of living; a splendid greatness. Therefore it is not capable of being scaled down successfully.

ANTHEMION   ACANTHUS LEAF

CHAPTER III

SPAIN

Spain was entirely Mohammedan until 1030 and in part for several centuries after that. Its art was cooler African; in the Moorish phase, as revealed by the Alhambra and the Giralda at Seville, it was a reflection of Persia, Arabia, Turkey and Morocco. Christianity was a reaction: Spain became a province of Italy, and Italian forms were worked by people with an undeniable Moorish strain. The result is a distinct type strongly parallel to the Italian.

The Gothic stage is marked by an austere functionalism; harsh and simple. Domestic decoration yielded in importance to the ecclesiastical.

The Renaissance brought Spanish influence and art to its zenith.

SPANISH RENAISSANCE

As Spain became a great power and felt its national pride, it rocketed upward into a brief commanding position in world affairs that did not end until the vast Spanish Armada was annihilated in 1588. During this time, Spain carved out an empire stretching from the Horn to the Columbia River, and, in the person of the Spanish Hapsburg emperor Charles V, offered a ruler whose sway reached over more territory than any Roman emperor, including Spain, Germany, Austria, the Netherlands, and Italy. It was inevitable that

27

such national importance should have engendered a distinctive architecture and furniture on a similar scale.

The 15th and 16th century Spaniard was cruel and proud, a conqueror who spurned ease and relaxation. Italian Renaissance furniture was interpreted in Spain in terms of rude massiveness and harsh simplicity. Ladies of royal and noble rank were expected to sit rigidly upright or retire to bed, while their arrogant lords planned further conquests. The room of Philip II, successor to Charles V, has been preserved, and gives us a court picture of the times. Plain plaster walls are barely relieved by a wainscot of blue and white tiling. Oak beams cross the ceiling; the doors are of somber oiled pine; the shutters are painted an austere green. The furniture is sparse and rugged. Spain regarded itself still as an armed camp; the luxury of the rest of Renaissance Europe was largely lacking.

17TH CENTURY SPANISH

The most noteworthy pieces were chairs, tables, benches, chests and vargueños, an article of furniture combining desk and cabinet. One type of chair was rectangular, with corded, stretched and nailed leather, or solid wooden seats, with tooled leather backs, and legs straight, grooved, carved or baluster, or spiral turned legs, with claw, scroll or turned feet. In Catalonia, they were often lacquered elaborately in green and red, with gold decorations. The other type of chair was a Spanish variant of the curved X, Savonarola, or Dante chair. With other pieces of furniture, this was often ornamented with carved geometrical designs, chiefly circles, chipped out in tiny half moons, or intricately inlaid in ivory, bone or boxwood—a Moorish survival.

Tables and benches show legs heavily turned and splaying outward, with bracing of curved and twisted iron. Chests were made primarily of oak, with rosette carvings, or with medallions containing profile portraits; at times they showed raised diamond-shaped Moorish panelling, similar to Tudor and Jacobean chests of the same century in England. The armories (armoires) of contemporary France appear in buffets and cupboards with arcaded spindles in the upper compartments, above the conventional high chest.

The vargueño, originating in royal Castile, had a huge front that hinged downward to form a writing desk when opened. Behind this stood a multitude of little-doored cabinets and drawers, often inlaid with geometrical, arabesque, or pictorial designs, in inlaid gold, silver, ivory, tortoise shell, bone or ebony. The upper exterior was often painted or lacquered in red or black. Often red velvet covered the front, overlaid with pierced lozenge-shaped Moorish plaques, of brass or gilded wood. The whole was set later upon intricate colonnaded legs.

18TH CENTURY SPANISH

The Spaniards preferred walnut in their furniture, with oak, chestnut and red pine next in popularity. The 18th century showed a swing to mahogany, a then new wood.

Fringed velvet and embossed leather coverings were held on with large round-headed nails, hammered in and crudely bent back on the reverse side.

Strong contrast is typical of all Spanish work. Highly decorated furniture is used against plain plaster walls, rich carpets on stone floors, brilliant offsets of high color against white or neutral grounds. Like the Italian, it requires size, airiness, open space. In modern work, the reproduction of Spanish interiors has been accomplished with highly theatrical effect but the style induced by the Florida boom of 1925 had little appropriateness and less skill. It scattered miniature Castillian palaces among our suburbs, and strained itself to become furniture unsuccessful in serving our needs or in reproducing a foreign atmosphere.

CHAPTER IV

FRANCE

Gothic architecture, superb in itself, offers little to the student of decoration. Its form is the essence of stone construction, and the complete harmony of architecture with all its allied arts grew out of the understanding of this construction. This example might well serve us today, now that we have a new structural form and method to develop.

French civilization rose on the groundwork of the Gothic. The five hundred years 1100 to 1600 saw the crumbling of feudalism and its replacement by a new social order. France became a nation but its birth was amid violence and brutality. The church was the basis of peace and security that fostered the arts; the various barons and princes were at each other's throats. Their houses were castles, fortresses; massive walls, small windows, a general brutality of solidity and space was the background for their few pieces of rude furniture. They had stone walls, stone floors, vaulted stone ceilings, or ceilings with heavy timber rafters, undecorated. Toward 1200, Flemish weavers began the manufacture of wool tapestries, and wainscot began to transform the walls, richly colored glass windows and other architectural features indicated the character of all decoration. Practically all furniture was architectural in concept and decoration, employing tracery, linen-fold

BENCH

FRENCH GOTHIC

31

LANTERN

BED POST.
FRENCH
RENAISSANCE.

panelling, and floral themes. There were tables, coffers, cupboards, chests, benches, and settles, a few chairs, but the organization of the room was rude and of too different a quality to be adapted to the contemporary scene.

FRENCH RENAISSANCE

The Renaissance filtered into France just as the Gothic had filtered into Italy. It arrived in bits and coalesced into a style. The French Renaissance, known by its kings, Charles VII, Francis I, Henry II, and others, came along with the improvement in secular life. Palaces and chateaus took more of the architects' attention. At first, occasional pieces of furniture wandered up into France; the suitable background followed. Rooms of the periods of Francis I, about 1530, exhibit clearly developed style . . . distinguished by classic grace, but full of unique carving and Italian motifs. Francis I built the chateaus at Blois, Chaulors, and Fontainebleau; they were on the grand scale and there is little important work of a lesser scale.

The later Renaissance was more purely Italian; the Florentine Catherine de Medici was the mother of Henry II, Charles IX and Henry III. The court was Italian; so were the artists and the architecture. Lesser nobles and gentry felt its influence. They had wealth, sureness, and a yearning for the grandeur of the Italian magnificoes. They borrowed what impressed them and planned their rooms to resemble their impressions of Italian rooms. Of course, they had to use local weavers, carvers and carpenters. Probably they explained in great detail just how they wanted their things to look; but what they achieved was distinctive and new. After

EARLY ITALIAN INTERIOR. FIREPLACE AND PAINTED WALLS ARE IN THE GOTHIC
MANNER; THE FURNITURE IS OF THE EARLY RENAISSANCE.

French & Company, Decorators.

DECORATED CEILING IN THE ELABORATE STYLE OF
THE MIDDLE RENAISSANCE; By Pintoricchio, 1588.
Metropolitan Museum of Art.

LIVING ROOM IN THE SPIRIT OF THE ITALIAN RENAISSANCE.
Mary Coggeshall - Jeannette Jukes, Inc., Decorators.

OLD ITALIAN ROOMS ADAPTED
TO MODERN LIVING.

•

Courtesy Alexander H. Girard.

THE EXUBERANT ITALIAN BAROQUE BEDROOM FROM THE
PALAZZO SAGREDO, VENICE, 1718.

The Bed and Dressing Table occupy a raised alcove at one end of the room. The larger part
of the room proper has the character of a sitting room.

Metropolitan Museum of Art

ITALIAN BAROQUE FURNITURE
IN MODERN SETTING.

Courtesy Bassett E. Vollum.

ITALIAN 18th CENTURY WALLPAPER.

ITALIAN ROCOCO. LATE 18th CENTURY.

MOTIVE, SCALE, FORM AND COLOR ARE BRILLIANT, CAPRICIOUS, DELICATE.
VARIATIONS OF LOUIS XV AND LOUIS XVI CHAIRS AND TABLES.

Photographs Courtesy Lavezzo, Inc.

WALNUT ARMCHAIR COVERED WITH
RED VELVET. 16th CENTURY.

WALNUT VARGUENO.
16th CENTURY.

WALNUT TABLE. 16th CENTURY.

CARVED CATALONIAN WALNUT CHEST.
17th CENTURY.

VARGUENO. (Closed)

SPANISH FURNITURE

Photographs Courtesy Montllor Brothers.

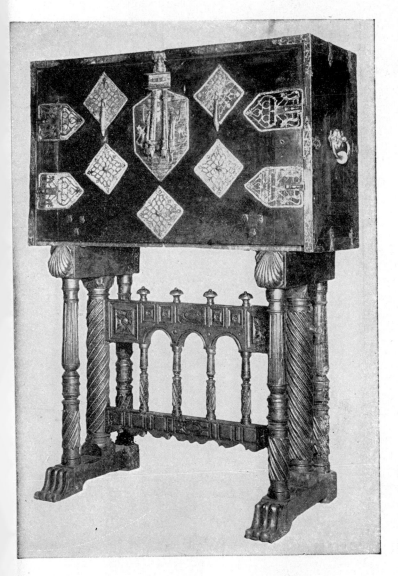

(Left) WALNUT CHAIR. 17th CENTURY.

(Right) CARVED WALNUT SIDEBOARD, 17th CENTURY.

SPANISH RENAISSANCE INTERIORS: HOUSE OF EL GRECO, TOLEDO.
Courtesy Hispanic Society of America.

A SETTING WITH FRENCH GOTHIC FURNITURE.
Courtesy French and Company.

GOTHIC FURNITURE ARRANGED WITH AN APPROPRIATE
ARCHITECTURAL BACKGROUND.

Courtesy French and Company.

LIBRARY IN WHITE AND GOLD

ROOMS FROM THE HOTEL DE GAULIN,
DIJON, 1772, STYLE OF LOUIS XVI.
Now in The Metropolitan Museum of Art.

BEDROOM WITH ALCOVE FOR BED.

FURNITURE, RUG, MANTEL AND ACCESSORIES OF THE PERIODS OF LOUIS XV
AND LOUIS XVI.

Courtesy Nancy McClelland, Inc. Photo Richard Averill Smith.

BEDROOM, CHATEAU DE MEREVILLE. PERIOD OF LOUIS XVI. PALE GREEN AND
CREAM WALLS, CREAM CARPET.

House of Sarah Hunter Kelly, Decorator. Photo F. S. Lincoln.

Photo F. S. Lincoln.

WALL PAINTING IN THE MANNER OF PILLEMENT. (STYLE OF LOUIS XVI).
CHAIRS AND CHEST ARE PROVINCIAL TYPES OF THE PERIOD.

Courtesy Ruth Campbell Bigelow, Decorator.

Louis XV Furniture

BEDROOM IN A FRENCH CHATEAU. WALLS COVERED WITH ORIGINAL TOILE DE JOUY.

"Replanting of The Gardens of Versailles," Designed by Hu[...] (Period of Louis XVI).

FRENCH FURNITURE OF THE DIRECTOIRE STYLE. (1795-1804).
Courtesy, Douglas Somerville Inc.
Reprinted by Permission of "The Decorator's Digest."

DIRECTOIRE WALL PAPER, GOLD AND MAUVE
ON GRAY BACKGROUND.

Courtesy Nancy McClelland.
All Photographs on this Page Reprinted by Permission
of "The Decorator's Digest."

EMPIRE SECRETAIRE.
AMBOYNA BURL WITH
ORMOLU MOUNTS.

(Wildenstein & Co.)

DIRECTOIRE TOILES DE JOUY.
Courtesy Elinor Merrill.

NAPOLEON'S DESK AND CHAIR
FROM FONTAINEBLEAU.

Courtesy, Dr. M. Therese Bonney.

FURNITURE OF THE DIRECTOIRE STYLE WITH A SUITABLY
DECORATED BACKGROUND.

French and Company, Decorators.

French and Company, Decorators

ROOM WITH ENGLISH GOTHIC ARCHITECTURAL DETAILS.
WITH FURNITURE OF SUBSEQUENT ENGLISH PERIODS.

EARLY ENGLISH LINENFOLD PANELLING.

Courtesy Stair and Andrew.

JACOBEAN FURNITURE WITH HARMONIZING BACKGROUND.

REGENCY CONSOLE TABLE.

CHIPPENDALE CHAIRS WITH
PETIT-POINT NEEDLEWORK SEATS.

Courtesy Vernay.

SHERATON SOFA TABLE AND MIRROR USED
AS A DRESSING TABLE.

SIDE CHAIR BY SHERATON, ABOUT 1800.
BLACK AND GOLD LACQUER.

a while they probably came to like it and decided that their interpretations were better than the originals.

The scale of most palace rooms was impressive, magnificent. The materials were costly; inlays of ebony, metals, and stone augmented the architectural display. Wood floors were covered with Oriental rugs; wool tapestries hung on the walls, which were decorated with semi-structural features—columns and ornate compositions. The fireplace was a tremendous, involved composition. The entire scale was gigantic and regal.

PROVINCIAL FRENCH

What is more significant is the growth of the lesser style during this time: the rich merchant and the burgher built smaller imitations of the court styles. The emergence of this class develops a certain native genius. Its work drops or distorts the foreign influence once it has had its start. Parallel to the familiar history of the royal palaces we must consider the lesser work. As we proceed further north on the map of France, we find the Italian influence less and less positive; local versions are surer. These interpret the people better and are a more interesting document. The group of styles is generally referred to as *Provincial French*. It is most interesting for its wide variety and a certain capacity for being mixed with other styles of similar origin. It is always significant that these provincial makers of furniture were not unduly excited when the king changed his mind about style; they continued to work in the good old way. They took only the superficial details of the Italian, because their houses in

Flanders and the north of France had a different duty from those of Italy.

There was one general quality in all these houses—a sense of being lived in. Whether in the north or the south, the domestic form of living room took on the characteristics by which we know such rooms. The planning was unconscious, and therefore direct; the decoration was a spontaneous affair, prompted in design by the material used and the degree of skill.

PROVINCIAL FRENCH

The typical articles of furniture in these middle class houses were cupboards, sideboards, tables, arm-chairs, benches and stools. They were soundly, honestly constructed (the law saw to that!). Oak was used more than walnut; iron fittings were cunningly made. Beds were architectural in idea; built-in boxes, a room within a room. One retired into this alcove, drew the curtains and spent the night in a pleasant state of semi-asphyxiation.

This was the state of furniture in France thru the 17th century: slowly evolving in the lower orders, while the upper crust seethed with new styles and influences according to the taste of the current monarch.

LOUIS XIII

Under Louis XIII the assimilative phase of the French Renaissance ended, the Italian Influence de-clined to the extent that the Baroque phase was a matter of local exaggeration. France had become a political unit. Rooms of this time exhibit a definite, individual style, in which the various imported types and influences were nicely balanced and set off against a background that was clearly French. The majestic features were no less grand, but they were coherent: the collection of objects had been succeeded by a highly organized homogeneous whole. Rich stuffs from the near East were supplemented by East Indian materials, the East India trade having been organized.

The king's cabinet maker, Laurent Stabre, was described as "joiner and carpenter in ebony," indicating the revolution in luxury carpentering in France. Before the colored woods came from the Americas, ebony was the fashion, glued upon blackened pearwood for strength and size. Ivory and bone were used to relieve the funereal sombreness of ebony. Inlays and mosaics include every conceivable substance below precious stones. The cabinets were incredibly ornate. Intricate tables of stone mosaic and gilt legs replaced previous simplicity. In these, in beds, everything, utility had given way to expensive foreign decoration and over-decoration. Turners replaced carvers.

Now that life had become less wandering, the cabinet replaced the portable coffer among fashionable folk. Tables had H-stretchers or X-stretchers joining the legs, intricately carved friezes, and drawers—chiefly rectangular, but also round, oval, or octagonal. The round table was popular, since it did away with all fine points of etiquette in seating. The extending table came in with the 16th century, as well as many folding tables. The bureau came in—its name from a fabric used to cover tables; then used for the table, especially as used to write on; and, as combined with a cabinet, the bureau we know today. The beds were hidden under incredible piles of fabrics. Chairs were low-backed, almost invariably. The rest-bed came in, the ancestor

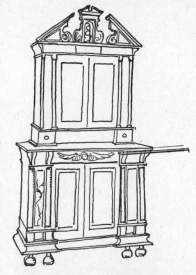

BED

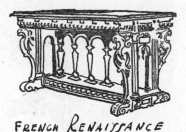

FRENCH RENAISSANCE

of many later pieces of furniture. Caned chair backs were foreign, and straw seats did not come in until later. The whole array of furniture was rather ponderous for modern living.

THE REGAL AGE OF LOUIS XIV

Louis XIV or Louis Quatorze furniture, alone among all the periods of man's house-furnishing, represents one man: Louis XIV, the Grand Monarch. There was a succession of lovely ladies who ruled over the court—de la Vallière, de Montespan, de Maintenon; but none of them ruled the king, as de Châteauroux, de Pompadour and du Barry dominated his successor and great-grandson, Louis XV. We could study his furniture and that of Louis XV's grandson, Louis XVI, who succeeded him, without noticing the king who lent his name to the style; but this is not true of the Grand Monarch. During the first half of his reign, he followed his armies; Le Brun, the king's pet architect and decorator, made his furniture tall, stiff and pompously warlike, during these years. As the boudoir became more important than the camp, a gentler note was introduced. But always it was the king who was the sun of everything.

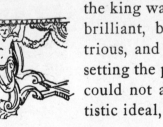

France at this time was the most powerful state in Europe, both in military power and in the arts; and the king was undisputed master of France. He was not brilliant, but he was infinitely energetic and industrious, and he ruled directly. France could not avoid setting the pattern for European furniture; and France could not avoid following docilely the king's one artistic ideal, which was that of magnificence. When the king determined to build at Versailles and Marely, the Louvre, Saint Germain, and Fontainebleau, regardless of expense, his minister Colbert secured for him the world's artisans and artists: Domenico Cucci, a cabinet-maker specializing in decorations of gold, bronze, colored stones, ornaments, figures; Philippe Caffieri, a sculptor in wood and metal; Charles Andre Boulle; Oppenord; Le Brun—hardly a Frenchman among them. The workshops of the Gobelins, under Le Brun, produced tapestries, fabrics, metal work, carved wood, silver work, frescoes. The result was the style of a king, not of a people.

The furniture of the merchants and gentlemen was still largely of the plain undisguised Louis XIII type. The peasants had, in the large, no furniture at all: they were described as "certain wild animals, male and female, scattered about the countryside," and wild animals have not risen to the dignity of furniture. The more opulent among them, especially those who served the royal and noble needs, had a plain coffer of two, a cupboard, a bed, benches, rude stools, a board for a table, a small mirror. Soon enough they all served for firewood.

Even during the age of Louis XIII, French art and furniture had been cosmopolitan. The age of Louis XIV assimilated everything into one regal cosmopolitan style.

This Louis was ambitious. He extended the control of the state—that is, his own—over the existing manufactories, and established others. The *Manufacture Royale Des Meubles De La Couronne* was organized under royal auspices to make furniture, tapestries, metal work and jewelry; the Gobelin factory and that of Beauvais made textiles and tapestries. Royal encouragement was given to painters and sculptors, landscapers, cabinet-makers, potters, lace-makers and every form of artistry and craftsmanship. The royal rooms fairly creaked with Art.

Ceiling painting was an enlargement of the classic extravagance of Italy; walls were painted with historical or legendary tableaux. The walls were also hung with allegorical tapestries—Valor and Conquest, Purity of the Passions, Progress of the Arts and Sciences. The same pompousness afflicted all forms of design and enlarged the scale of everything pertaining to decoration. Tremendous vases of Sevres on marble-top tables, huge pier glasses, enormous articles of furniture—maintained a certain ostentatious dignity. Patterns of fabrics were necessarily expanded. Early 16th century fabrics had small detached floral motives; at the end of the century these had become intertwined floral-architectural ornaments.

This style produced the widest variety of fabrics. Brocatelles and brocades, satins, silks and damasks, embroideries, fabrics with metal threads were part of the scheme. It is curious to note that printed fabrics were popular enough to threaten more serious textiles. In 1686 Minister Colbert prohibited the manufacture or importation of printed linen; yet it was bootlegged even into Madame Pompadour's Bellevue. Papers followed fabrics on walls as the degree of importance diminished. The Domino papers of Italy, small marbleized squares, were probably pasted on some wall or other in every house in Paris about 1700. True wall paper came in from China during Louis XIV's reign and the Chinese themes persisted even in the domestic copies.

The furniture was ornate, massive, rich. This was especially true of the work of the famous cabinet-makers, Boulle and his four sons.

Contact with China had been reestablished, and every house had to have its plethora of Chinese articles and ornamentations. Louis XIV was very proud of his Chinese cabinet with ten silver plaques representing the labors of Hercules. Such was the taste of the Grand Monarch and his obsequious age. Chinese porcelain and Delft faience were everywhere. The straight line was most obvious, especially at first; brief curved lines appeared, but never with the sense of loosened languor of the Louis XV style. Complicated panels were classic in outline, often with the Gothic crow's bill ornamentation. Allegorical furniture became popular, with the King as Apollo, and Maria Theresa as Diana; there are Cabinets of Glory, of Virtue, of Peace, of War. . . . Simple masques and grotesque *mascarons* were constantly used. There were lions, rams, stags, the monsters of mythology, the scallop shell that played such a part in *Venus Rising from the Sea*; there were endless ancient weapons used in the decorations, always in infinite symmetry. Colors were violent and unharmonious. Gilt spread over all of the furniture. Glittering magnificance was everywhere preferred to the simple strength and beauty of walnut and oak. Marquetry or inlay used almond and box for yellow, holly for blank white, pearwoods for red, walnuts for browns ranging to black, Saint Lucia Wood for pinkish gray.

And shading with fire gave all the grades of these. Brass, pewter, tortoise-shell, and colorless horn painted gaudily on the under side, completed the rainbow. Glue bound the whole together; and metals did not take kindly to glue, and damp undid the rest.

Cupboards, sideboards, bookcases, and commodes were tortured with constant panelling. Furniture for the first time became stationary, and the coffer for transporting goods lost all importance. The bookcase cupboard, called soon the bookcase, grew in response to the spread of printed books. The ornate cabinet disappeared during this period. The commode appeared first about 1700, called the bureau-commode at first; in 1718 the queen-mother defined it merely as "a large table with drawers," although others derived it from an altered chest. Massive plump three-drawer commodes were later softened into the lovely Regency commode. Most amazing of all were commodes in brass and tortoise-shell marquetry with four drawers, rectangularly simple and appallingly over-decorated.

Beds were so monumental that most of them were destroyed as soon as the taste for smaller beds came in. Completely covered up with costly embroideries, fringes, cords, gold tassels, and plumes, they had no independent artistic value. The state bed often cost more than all the rest of the furniture combined. It and the carriage marked the family wealth, as the silver anklets of a Hindu coolie wife constitute the family fortune. Every sort of bulwark against the cold was used. There were thirty-three distinct textile parts of the complete bed, which surely made it complicated enough. The plumes were precisely like those on modern hearses, except for their color: the four groups were composed of a hundred ostrich feathers, disposed around aigrettes of heron feathers, and colored as gaily as the bed hangings. These were state beds, in which many a lady of fashion reclined, fully clothed, while receiving guests. Moliere's bed had eagle feet in green bronze, and an azure dome, carved and gilt—the imperial bed, as it was called. Tomb beds had lower foot posts, and sloped downward, giving less air to the sleepers. Angel-beds and duchess-beds lacked the four posts.

Rest-beds, ancestors of the chaise longue and the sofa, appeared in the time of Mazarin, and were common during the time of Louis XIV. Tables became more elaborate, inlaid and gilded, usually topped with costly marble, porphyry, alabaster, or "Florence tables" of many-colored stone mosaic. Some placed against a wall had only three sides decorated; and were called console tables, from their resemblance to the architectural consoles that were so popular. The curved doe's foot leg became more and more popular. There were innumerable specialized tables, especially for gaming. Toilet-tables and night-tables appeared toward the end of the reign. The writing-table emerged, and out of it the bureau, culminating in the imposing *scribanne* or desk-cupboard.

Etiquette permitted a duchess to sit in an armchair, until the king entered the room; whereupon she was at once to move to a stool; as ladies below the rank of duchesses had to quit the stools, and sit upon hassocks. The imposing Louis XIV armchairs seem designed to accommodate the noble's peruke and ribboned costume, or the woman's high rayed headdress. The backs are higher than the width, unlike the lower-backed Louis XIII chairs. Heavy stretchers joined the legs at the base. Middle class chairs followed the same lines, but without carvings and mouldings. "Confessional" chairs, later called bergeres, came in during this reign, at first for priests to sit at ease in, while listening to confessions. Low-backed chairs, including those called "gossips," came in toward the end of the reign. And the sofa emerged, as a revived more comfortable bench. Caned chairs were imported from Holland or Flanders about 1690.

REGENCE

During the last years of Louis XIV's reign, Philip Duke of Orleans was regent and the furniture of the period from about 1710 to 1735 is known as the Regency style. Its characteristic feature is the modification of Louis XIV forms. This change is noticeable mostly in ornament and this mostly in the flat curved panelling. There was the curve at the corners and the foliage-and-ribbon ornamentation. The latter ornament affected furniture which used it as such. But besides, curved legs replaced straight ones. The curve was slight, having the contour of a cross-bow; this slight curve and cross-bow also characterized upper members of the book cases and cabinets. Thin bronze mouldings and frames paralleled the gentle lines of these curves.

Chairbacks had pierced carving consisting of the distinctive foliage and ribbons, and the commodes newly developed were slightly bulging (bombe).

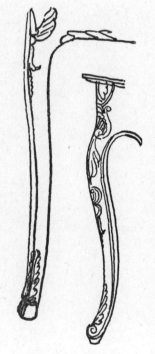

DOE'S FOOT
LOUIS XIV

Ebony veneer was superseded by polished walnut, mahogany and rosewood veneers.

The artistic value of Regency furniture lies in its blending of artistic restraint with delicate movement. Charles Cressent was the leading cabinet-maker of this period.

The color schemes of the successive periods are our best key to the changing emotional states. Louis XIV was an ambitious politician; color as well as light and shade was strong, masculine, ebullient. The rich pomp of deep toned walls, whether fabric or otherwise, was a foil for the brilliance of gold and gilding, bronze, variegated marbles, porcelains, Oriental carpets. The colors were always full bodied, reds were winey, blues intense, greens solid and grass colored. They are suave but not subtle. The Regency softened and feminized these schemes; it made more of group and subdued tones. The complicated palette of Louis XV employed pastel tones and reduced contrasts; tints and shades were preferred to contrasts; white and gold were chosen for elegance. Reds became rose or pink; greens, grays, blues were all chalky, with gold trim.

CHAPTER V

FRANCE: AFTER LOUIS XIV

THE FEMININE FURNITURE OF LOUIS XV

The age of Louis XV was the heyday of curved wood and other feminine touches suitable for a frivolous and voluptuous period, sanctifying debauchery. After fifteen years the style became Rocaille (derisively nicknamed Rococo), from the use of shells and rocks decoratively. The style is curved and capricious, with a horror of straight lines and symmetry. Wood is naturally comparatively straight and not curved, and had to be tortured into this feminine curvature.

Below the court furniture, farms and homesteads began to acquire huge simple cupboards, metal-fitted dressers, cherry armchairs upholstered in colored linen —sound solid work, with a return to favor of oak and walnut, straw chairs—all with far more beauty than the court pieces. But the typical Louis XV furniture is marked by the curving character of all the lines, especially those legs like an elongated *S,* called doe's feet—at first terminating in a deer's cleft foot, with a line suggesting a deer's hind leg. Rocaille, a name first for an artificial outdoor grotto decorated with queer stones and shells, was applied about 1800 to the art of the period. The style was a violent reaction against the severity of Louis XIV; but it usually lacked the typical French qualities of restraint, balance, clarity, and reason.

Charles Cressent continued to be the important cabinet-maker but his work paralleled the change in style. Ornaments of gilded bronze or ormolu pervaded his work, all in hectic artistry. Jean Francois Oeben, the "king's cabinet-maker," was king of the *ebenistes* —for cabinet-makers were still proudly called ebony-workers. The Marquise de Pompadour, with her innumerable houses to furnish, was his chief patron— not the king. She had taste and a liking for simple works; but the current against Louis XIV was too strong for her. Critics at last became abundant, and furniture came under classic influences about 1763. Thus the style of Louis XVI was born some dozen years before his accession.

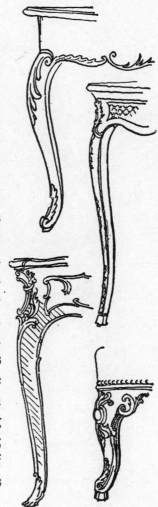

Furniture was restored at last to convenient human size. Comfort and intimacy replaced frigid magnitude. Little rooms for conversation, play and music appeared, each calling for appropriate furniture. A Louis XV house was obviously easy to live in. Wall and other decoration became intimate, rather than solemn and forbidding. France became one huge boudoir. Light chairs and cabriolet seats replaced the stiff unyielding wall thrones. Sofas, ottomans, easy-chairs, chaise longues, *duchesses* and *veilleuses* promised and gave comfort. Tea-tables, toilet-tables, and countless more appeared. The curved line was at least the line of nature, if not the nature of wood; furniture began to have "an agreeable contour." There was a flowing unity and continuity of all the parts of furniture; furniture looked as if it were cast in one piece; as if wood had been melted into metal. And symmetry was avoided like the pox.

There was no lack of art in this asymmetry. It is more difficult to balance equivalent masses than identical masses; yet this was achieved. The decorative motifs included an asymmetrical scallop-shell, the bean, the lozenge, the cartouche, the natural garland, flowers placed with random artistry, pairs of amorous doves, Cupids, hearts, pastoral figures and symbols, musical instruments, dervishes, odalisques, sultanas: the symbols of a boudoir, not of victory in tourney or battle. Chinamen and monkeys were used indiscriminately. Decoration was to relax the mind, for a frivolous and gallant age.

Native woods were still used—oak, walnut, cherry, solid beech, elm, fruit-tree woods. In 1725 huge blocks of mahogany from Haiti and Honduras began to come in—the most valuable varieties being those whose veining was "thorny," "flaming," "watered," and "speckled." Mahogany was the wood preeminently for carving. With it came that wine-red or dark violet mahogany called amaranth, and satinwood, both red and yellow. These became popular in the South of France even before they reached Paris. Not only panels, but whole articles of furniture, were brilliantly inlaid, to form elaborate pictures in the taste of Boucher, even with dyed woods to complete the palette. Painted furniture was popular, either "flatted" or lacquered (varnished). Vivid colors were the rage. The four brothers Martin were most distinguished for their lacquering in the Chinese manner, succeeding equally well in a snuff-box or a whole suite of rooms. These became the symbol of the most refined luxury.

Bureaus and writing desks were topped with replaceable morocco leather; consoles, commodes, night-tables and others liable to be wet had marble tops, or exquisite natural coloration. Mosaics still were used, as well as cheap stucco imitations of these. Medallions of china came in. For the first time mirrors were set into bureaus and secretaries for ladies, into low book-shelves, and wardrobe fronts,—though not as mirror-doors. Wardrobes became second in importance only to beds—their immense size being their chief fault. The corner-cupboard was invented, and the under-cup-board. In Arles, in Provence, the credence-sideboard was invented, a small cupboard set upon a huge base, whose uncovered top was convenient as a sideboard during meals. Dresser-sideboards became popular; and secretaries came in as an invention of about 1750, con-sisting of a front that let down into a writing table, with compartments or drawers above.

The commode, or chest of drawers, is the most typical piece of Louis XV furniture. There were many styles leading up to the chiffonnier, a tall piece with five drawers, appearing about 1750. The types of tables were legion, all marked by the doe's feet legs. Even peasant kitchen tables tended toward this court design, in crude and peasant-like manner: a much elongated *S*-shape, in finer specimens terminating in cases of gilded bronze, a volute on a cube, or an adapted doe's foot. The large dining-tables were so unwieldy that practically none of them have been preserved. The dumb-waiter was a little round table with superposed shelves and a wine-cooler above. The chiffonniere was a sort of sewing table, with a three-sided gallery on top; drawers, and shelf at the bottom enclosed in high

Louis XV
Decorations

network, for balls of wool. There were kidney-tables
—crescent-shaped or bean-shaped—designed for more
intimate comfort. There were gracefully designed
dressing-tables in the bedrooms, toilet-tables in "butter-
fly," and corner toilet-tables. Many had castors, to permit their being moved around, at a time when these
were rare.

The typical chair was the comfortable bergere, soft
and low, restful as a bed, upholstered in gay flowered
silk. The seats were all portable, since etiquette was
laid by for intimacy. The legs were always curved, and
the backs low. Most of these were "fiddle-backed"—
that is, slightly contracted about halfway up. Little
padded cushions on the arms were the thing: anything
for added comfort. The design was accommodated to
the panniered skirts of the ladies. Chairs for writing
desks were of the low "gondola" type. Velvet and
damask were chiefly used for upholstery, with taffeta
for summer use, in the form of slip-covers. Satin and
moire were also used. Cane chairs, often with the trellis
gilded, and strawchairs *a la capucine,* roughly turned
and put together, followed the general design of the
other chairs. Chaise longues and sofas were perfected,
as ideally suited to an intimate period. As before, few
beds have been preserved, for they were mainly crude
carpentry disguised by voluminous hangings. Screens
became smaller, or were reduced to the proportions of
fire-screens. They were often covered with fabric or
wall-paper, and sometimes had mirrors set into the
upper part.

The century before had seen the invention of the
tall clock, to accommodate the weights, even before the

invention of the pendulum which caused an expansion just below the center of the case. Typical clocks were intricately decorated with bronze, and had the typical feminine lines of the period. Mirror and picture frames were carved, not made of plaster, and were dignified and impressive, with an ornate capital at the top. Even in this, the curved lines of the boudoir age were often preserved.

THE CLASSIC REVIVAL UNDER LOUIS XVI

Shortly after 1754, France discovered the ruins of Greece, in a series of works on the arts of ancient Greece and Italy. From 1748 on, buried Herculaneum and Pompeii seized the imagination of the French mind, now less sure of itself and eager for a model to follow. And shortly articles in the Greek manner appeared and the Louis XVI style had begun. Architecture responded first; then tiny decorations; and finally furniture—first the decorations, and then the design itself. In 1754 the first published criticism against the style of Louis XV appeared, based on the lack of good sense and excess of imagination; the overuse of complicated curves; and the mania for vegetable ornament. By 1764, a line in a comedy announced, "Everything is Greek, except our souls." And, since they were not Greek of soul, the cabinet-makers had the wisdom to remember this in their designings. While the upper classes play-acted, not at being the amorous shepherds of the age of Louis XV, but idling Greek gods, the volcano rumbled beneath them, until a more permanent eclipse than that which overwhelmed Pompeii and Herculaneum darkened forever all they stood for.

The chief cabinet-maker of the period was Jean Henri Riesener, by birth a German. His compositions in furniture are marked by ample grandeur, exquisitely proportioned, and in the best sense of the word architectural; yet they never lose the graceful supple line. Marie Antoinette adored roses; Riesener worked chiefly for her; roses are one of his chief motifs of decoration: so styles come. But even the roses are exquisite, and other pieces have a masculine strength. He translated antiquity into living French forms, as Pope translated Homer into couplets polished like the wits of his age. Jean-Francois Leleu, Claude Charles Saunier, Etienne Avril, banished flowers, knots or ribbons, even inlay or marquetry. David Roentgen—another German—retained marquetry among these, but was as classically severe as they otherwise. As the deluge approached, the classic taste became more severe.

Architecture moved toward the strict Doric of the temple of Poseidon at Paestum; and furniture decoration kept pace with it. The boudoir of Marie Antoinette at Fontainebleau had little Greek decorations. There is a kinship between this art and that of the regal Louis XIV period: the origin was the same.

Just as each successive style grows during the preceding period, transition forms appear linking this period and Empire, with tripod tables supported by caryatids and tables whose legs are surmounted by sphinx heads.

The age of Louis XVI was an age satiated with worldly pleasure-seeking, and a willingness to dip superficially into simplicity, virtue and reason. The

noble and simple beauty of antiquity had to be shaped
into the licentiousness that upper-class France had become. Greece was mainly seen through Roman eyes, of
course; the Roman line began to rule furniture. Symmetry returned, and severe borders defining undecorated surfaces. The beauty of classic proportions was
repeatedly caught in article after article; although the
intended use was not classic, except in the more de-
graded sense. Column, volute, Roman eagle, dolphins,
animal heads, accurate doe's feet, mythological monsters in profusion, classic vegetation, especially the
acanthus leaf, elegant masks derived from the Greek
comic and tragic masks, the pomegranate, the thyrsus
of the Bacchante, the caduceus of Hermes, bows,
quivers, urns, tripods—all the trappings of antiquity
decorated France just before the Revolution.

The chairs compromised with the previous style by
being straight in leg and back, and curved at the sides
and in front. Chair arms were awkwardly accommodated to the voluminous panniers, which women increasingly wore. When panniers disappeared, the arms
began with projections of the front legs, a style difficult to render graceful. Hollowed-out chair backs were
called cabriolet backs; were often oval in shape; and
decorated at the top with a bow of ribbon design, as
if the chairback were an oval frame for hanging. Comfortable bergeres, including the confessional-shaped,
were still in use. Among the most popular design for
wooden-backed chairs was the lyre. Straw-seated chairs
became more elegant, and at times were provided with
cushions. Chaise longues were made in one piece, two
equal pieces, two unequal pieces, or three pieces—

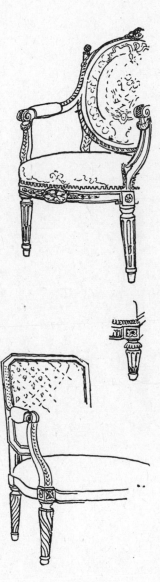

two bergeres and a square stool with hollowed sides into which the bergeres fitted closely.

Beds had become smaller, with visible decorated wood, and hence are more often found. The shapes were innumerable—the Polish, the imperial, the Italian, the Turkish, as well as new shapes, the Panurge, the military, the Chinese. The four-poster bed returned to favor. Angel-beds, meant to be seen end-wise, and amply decorated in painted wood, were popular. Screens carried out the general design; clocks were ornamented "after the Greek."

THE ANTIQUE EMPIRE STYLE

There was no real Directoire (Directory) style, since the Directors governed only four years altogether. The first effect of the Revolution on furniture was the addition of Revolutionary emblems to the decoration of Louis XVI pieces: symbols of liberty, triumphal arches, Liberty caps, spirit levels, pikes, oaken boughs, clasped hands, tables of the law, and the capture of the Bastille carved on cupboards. Imitation of the antique began to run wild. General Napoleon's little mansion, purchased after his Italian campaign, had furniture bedizened with symbols of war and victory: stools that were drums, with their cords stretched around a barrel of yellow hide; a mahogany commode with lions' heads; a bureau ornamented with Roman glaives or spearheads.

The Egyptian campaign of Napoleon, which had been accompanied by archeologists and artists, brought in a fit of Egyptomania. Vivant-Denon, an architect-archeologist who had been taken along, had a Pharonic

bedroom designed, its bed ornamented on three sides
with bas-reliefs of rows of kneeling figures, a carved
Isis at its head, the legs showing the upright cobra
symbol. There were bedrooms that were soldiers' tents,
with hangings held up by pikes; with weapons, spears
and shields everywhere; with the bedposts surmounted
by Greek helmets. When Napoleon became Consul,
he at once set the artists to restoring and furnishing
Josephine's Malmaison. Percier and Fontaine were
employed for this purpose; they turned next to refit-
ting Saint Cloud, the Tuileries, the Louvre, and the
rest. Not that Napoleon was artistic; but he felt the
wisdom of having his background a solid and grandiose
luxury, to impress the world with his power. David,
Percier and Fontaine were the creators of the official
Empire Style. Their architectural achievement may
be unacceptable now, but it was appropriate to the
hour.

France was now an armed camp, armed against the
world. Her furniture and decoration, of broad austere
surfaces, marked out by straight lines and sharp edges,
displayed swords and triumphal palms, with golden
Victories postured with widespread wings. They
ignored the Greek lesson of making Victory wingless,
that it might never fly away. This was not an indigenous
French style, but a style exhumed by antiquarians.
It never expressed the French soul, but in Napoleon's
hour, it spread enthusiastically through the nations.

The motto of French Empire was to achieve the
opposite of the Ancient Regime in every particular,
for all that Empire stemmed directly out of the classic
revival under Louis XVI. Percier and Fontaine ac-

POMPEIIAN

cepted everything in antiquity pell-mell, without distinction, Egyptian, Greek, Etruscan, Roman, indiscriminately, from the Parthenon down to the decorations of the Street of the Lupanars in Pompeii. It was antique, therefore logical, beautiful, and not to be improved upon. Not that there was any return to Spartan antique simplicity of furnishing or living: but luxurious French living had to be tricked out in ornate antique designs, as if in truth an Alexander or a Caesar had come again to a prostrate ancient world. Antiquity was seen as an age of melodramatic eloquence, and was interpreted so. Comfort, intimacy, grace and gaiety, vanished overnight; the leaders of the Empire movement worked in the grand style, severe and heroic. Curves vanished: square columns took their place. Symmetry became a god: as Fontaine worded it, "Simple lines, pure contours, correct shapes replacing the miscelinear, the curving and the irregular." As Roederer wittily wrote in 1802, "A thousand precautions are needed to avoid being bruised by the most gentle use of your furniture." It was the acme of the uncomfortable.

The Louis XVI period adopted from the antique only what was adaptable, without impairing the comforts of contemporary living; the Empire sought pure abstract beauty, ignoring comfort completely. This artificial rebellion against life and nature could not last. Frantic caryatids, human and monstrous, supported tables and the arms of armchairs; lion heads with huge chests above a huger paw were common. Gilt bronze decorated the vast flat surfaces of dark polished mahogany. Utility was disguised as completely as possible in everything.

Bronze decorations were in flat gilt. Classic Wedgwood plaques in white biscuit on a blue ground were the rage. Marquetry was out of favor, but inlaying was often used. Nearly all the tables were round, following classic examples, with all the monsters of mythology acting as caryatids to support them. The beds have no distinction between head and foot. "Boat beds" came in, to be placed in alcoves, with only one side visible; and this determined their architecture. The whole style was in revolt against all the recent past; and it can no more amalgamate in a room with furniture from that past than a Bonaparte and a Bourbon. A table centered the room, a Turkey carpet might be permitted, though bare floors were more "antique"; a piano-forte might appear as a costly novelty, though a harp was omnipresent.

Mahogany was infinitely more popular than any of the native woods, and ebony reappeared after its exile under Louis XV. Painted furniture was the rage. Plaques of Sevres china and Wedgewood biscuit ware were used in profusion, usually with classic motifs. In the provinces, the new classic mode progressed sluggishly, at best resulting in unhappy compromises between the two styles—the feminine modern French of Louis XV, the translated classic of Louis XVI. One new piece of furniture, the vitrine, a small cupboard or under cupboard, was invented, to house bric-a-brac; otherwise the furniture was the old pieces with classic outlines and decorations.

Tables had vertical legs and straight lines, and no

festoons; though smaller tables retained the doe's foot elongated *S* design. Cross-pieces between the legs reappeared. The jardiniere table, often decorated with Sevres plaques, came in.

The architectural background of rooms displayed again the rectangular quality of Louis XIV, but thinner, lighter, smaller. Symmetrical panellings with delicate mouldings were painted severely, and ornamental swags, ribbons and garlands were carefully restrained and framed-in. Mantels, doorways, and window frames were rectangular, simply architectural. Walls and detail were generally painted, using soft grays, and greens, gray blues and chalky pinks. The fabrics were most characteristically silk—damasks, and brocades, stripes and moirés, small patterned velvets are frequent, and printed fabrics were extremely popular. These were in the classic architectural forms; the Toile de Jouy was the product of a factory at Jouy near Versailles, operated by a German named Oberkampf. Walls were frequently covered with fabrics, or wall papers resembling fabric, but such decorations were usually set in panels.

The background of this excessively architectural furniture harmonized to the extent of employing all the structural symbols—columns, pilasters, arches, and panels, whenever possible. The color effects were deeper, more masculine. Mahogany was stained a deep reddish color, with strong greens, yellows and blues in vigorous shades as offsets. Trimming was usually metal or metal color. Fabrics on walls continued to be used and great panels were painted on plaster or canvas and framed in with mouldings.

The influence of Napoleon waned with his passing from the political scene. The succeeding years in France were as eclectic in style as in politics. Some elements of the Baroque and the Empire were most persistent, but they were applied as detail only; architecturally the world was at sea. The Industrial Revolution created a new wealthy class, aesthetically raw: the political tides swept in a new aristocracy. Nothing through the nineteenth century was settled except the kind of smug self-satisfaction of the new rich in France or elsewhere. The procession of styles from Empire through the Classic and Gothic revivals, the styles of Louis Philippe and the Third Empire, Art Nouveau and Art Moderne were generally unsuccessful efforts to harmonize new times and processes, new methods and new machines. In Gothic times the individual was liege to the church; when the church was superseded by the temporal, political power, he was the subject of kings. Throughout the 19th century the absolutism of kings waned and the man could not decide whose subject he was, or who was to set him his tune. The appearance of his home reflected this uncertainty.

CHAPTER VI

ENGLAND

THE AGE OF OAK : GOTHIC AND RENAISSANCE FURNITURE

England, from whom America most directly derived its furniture, was a little island west of Europe, constantly conquered and constantly absorbing its conquerors, until it emerged slowly to be the world power it is today. Channel, sea and ocean separated it from Europe at first as thoroughly as the ocean separates Australia from the rest of the world today. Its early Celts or Britons were conquered successively, but never wiped out, by Romans, Teutons (Angles, Saxons, and Jutes), Danes, and Normans. For centuries it sought, and almost succeeded, in ruling France; it let France go, to become the only empire owning land in every continent man has discovered. Gothic architecture and furniture had run their course in Italy in the 14th century; in Spain, in the 15th; in France, in the 16th; their influence was still strong in England at the end of the 17th century, after Tudor, Elizabethan, Jacobean, Commonwealth and Restoration had come and gone. There was no such simple succession of Gothic, Renaissance, Baroque, Classic, with minor variations, that the rest of Europe knew: there was one great English style of oak, that lasted until the Glorious Revolution of 1688, when Dutch William and Mary replaced Scotch-Frenchified Stuarts as sovereigns and walnut replaced oak. The Hanoverian Germans replaced the Dutch as rulers and lastly there was a period of French influence and mahogany replaced walnut. The decline came with the pervading eclecticism or pick-your-choice style, of the 19th century. This the antiquarians of Napoleon brought in restricted to antiquity, and it was soon broadened to include every style of every period from every land. In English decoration it is known as Victorianism.

The Norman Conquest (1066 A. D.) brought a piratical luxury and refinement. English homes that yielded to the Norman influence—as many did not—introduced more rooms, and such furniture as armories, cupboards, Romanesque or pre-Gothic chairs and chests, designed in France and Italy. Panel work and coloring, decorative historical painting, Oriental rugs and carpets, rich stuffs to cover bedroom furnishings, came in. It is common to say that the Renaissance reached England during the time of Elizabeth: and surely its intellectual and literary eddies did. But England was too wedded to its Celtic and Saxon past to accept this slavish imitation of filtered classicism. The English never fell under the Renaissance spell until Dutch walnut and French mahogany replaced the native oak, far in the future.

In the Norman (Romanesque) and early Gothic period in England, the unit of the home—the minimum, sometimes the all—was the great hall, used for all purposes. Stone walls covered with tapestries or arras kept out the cold and draughts. Floors were of earth or stone, covered with rushes. Tables were boards on stretchers, with boards to keep the feet off the ground. Retainers, dogs, and the like, sat, ate, drilled and slept in the great hall. The lord and his lady slept in a great curtained bed. Later, retiring rooms were provided for the women, which ultimately were placed up a stairway, imitating Oriental harem models seen by the Crusaders on their eastward journeyings. The styles were less palatial and more domestic than those of Europe. England had a more settled organization from the first than France or Italy; but her culture was cruder.

TUDOR AND ELIZABETHAN

Tudor, cresting in influential Henry VIII, came in, the English version of Gothic, with oak used almost exclusively for furnishings. With Elizabeth, Spanish and Italian Renaissance began to affect the Gothic. But England overwhelmed Spain in the destruction of the Armada, and she was no artless Rome to borrow her arts from conquered Spain, as Rome did from abject Greece. The Norman (Romanesque) and Gothic furniture in England was painted, in bright colors; and much ornamented by hangings, valances and cushions of rich gay materials. The painting was done in tempera or wax, and has largely disappeared. The armories held armor and liveries, and are architectural —internal representations of the buildings themselves. Rooms were panelled in rich vermilion, olive and dark green painted designs. The garde-robe (wardrobe) at first was a small adjoining room, and later a cupboard: it should never be forgotten that any of the functions of furniture may properly be built into the walls, as was often done in ancient as well as modern times. Intricately carved hutches, or chests or coffers on legs, often with medallions of their owners, were important pieces of furniture. The chest or coffer was the most important permanent article of furniture; for there was still need of moving one's furniture to the place one visited and protecting it from theft and vandalism, though conditions were always more settled than on the continent. The linenfold motif, taken from the chalice napkin covering the Eucharist host, was common.

The credence or buffet came in from France. It had the place of honor in the living room; although English credences were never as elaborate as French models. Chairs, as on the continent, derived, not from the Greek *thronos* for sitting purposes exclusively, but from chests with sides and back elevated, retaining the chest beneath the seat; and they were personal to the lord and lady of the house. *X* chairs came in, a remote derivation from classic models. Conversational chairs (*cacqueteuse* or *chaise de femme*) are occasionally found; but these never became popular. Chests were used for seating, often cushioned; as the larger chests, covered with a mattress, could be used for beds.

The crude room of medieval England was transformed during the Tudor reigns into a thing of great architectural pretense. Interior woodwork grew from the simple panelling of 1200 to a degree realized nowhere else. The architectural background of Renaissance England was the room—it needed no other decoration. Ceilings in Gothic work of exposed beams were now commonly finished in plaster, with elaborate interlacing patterns in less relief. The fireplace in chilly

England is a most vital affair; throughout the Tudor and Jacobean times it was a colossal structure of carved stone and wood, floor to ceiling. Windows were large, to admit a maximum of the wan light, but the outdoors could be excluded by great draw curtains of heavy fabrics.

Floors of rooms for public use were covered with rushes until a late date, but in the more private rooms the floors had Oriental carpets soon after the Crusades. It was an age of embroidery, wool, linen and cotton were worked into the decorative floral patterns of Crewel. In richer work more elegant stuffs were employed, silks and velvets were imported and treasured; deep reds and browns, greens and yellows harmonized easily with the omnipresent oak. Wide enthusiasm for all types of textiles caused the importation of weavers from France, Italy and Flanders. James I established the Mortlake tapestry factory; weaving communities settled in many cities and grew in importance.

Mirrors during Elizabeth's reign were imported and rare, and merited rich frames. Venetian mirror makers settled in England in 1685, and their product became more widespread, but the mirror frame remained traditional.

Following the custom of the monks, permanent refectory tables replaced mere boards; although even these at first could be knocked down and placed against the wall. Tables and, later, benches had bulbous turnings, and heavy designs. Cabinets for storage developed slowly, with intricate marquetry work. The cabinets included intricate writing table flaps. The beds were of a design older than French Gothic—a tester of wood surmounted by a cornice, and supported on a panelled back, with posts at each corner. The Great Bed of Ware, 10 feet 9 inches square and 7 feet 6½ inches high, could support four couples with ease. Later all this woodwork was covered with fabric, and the woodwork deteriorated. Joint-stools were popular, and triangular chairs of turned wood introduced from Byzantium into Scandinavia were brought into England by the Normans.

As early as 1557, the pseudo-classic style of using human, animal or monstrous caryatids to support tables was intermittently introduced. Lions' heads were carved on cupboards, and caryatids or supporting human figures bent beneath the weight of buffets above them. Sideboards of two tiers and a foot tier—three carved shelves supported by carved legs—began to appear. Draw tables, heavily supported, replaced mere boards. Henry VIII's fantastic castle of Nonesuch dominated furniture decoration until Charles II presented the palace to his mistress Barbara Palmer, whom he named Duchess of Cleveland and Baroness of Nonesuch; whereupon she sold the building and had it destroyed for the value of its materials.

JACOBEAN

Jacobean furniture was as heavy, and more ornate. The beds became mere studies in tapestried disguise over poor woodwork. Over-decoration accompanied the sterility of design. Soon enough the woodwork was largely invisible, being covered by comfortable cushions and stuffs,—a cruder method of achieving the **petticoat** comfort of the French style of Louis XV.

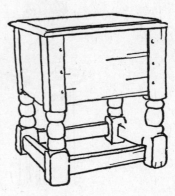

Coffee arrived as a drink in 1645, chocolate in 1657, tea in 1658—and this caused the invention of countless tables to serve these on.

The Revolution of 1649 was the climax of years of religious strife. The Puritans of the Revolution are the Puritans of Plymouth; the style upon which New England Colonial grew is also the style of Cromwell's England. In the ten years of Cromwell's domination, the Puritans saw it their duty to destroy as much as possible of the elegant pretentiousness of Charles' England: what they built was simple and sturdy but uncompromisingly austere and uncomfortable.

The pseudo-classic style is often referred to as the English Renaissance. The woods used in the marquetry inlaying were chiefly walnut, ebony, rosewood, pear, cherry, apple, box, ash, yew and holly. The pieces were strong and honest in construction compared to European models. At best it was Renaissance decoration superimposed upon a framework of sturdy English Gothic. Jacobean furniture, during the reign of the Scotch-English James I and Charles I, was less grandiose, smaller, more domestic, and with more evenly distributed ornamentation. The great English architects, Inigo Jones and Sir Christopher Wren, were the chief architectural sponsors of this revived classicism in England, corresponding to the periods of Louis XV and XVI in France.

After the end of the Protectorate, the restoration of the Stuarts brought in Late Jacobean or Restoration furniture, under Charles II and James II. The people looked with equal tolerance upon Stuart antics and mistresses, and the importation of French furniture

PILGRIM FURNITURE MAY HAVE BEEN IMPORTED BY THE COLONISTS,
OR MADE FROM ENGLISH MODELS. MIDDLE 17th CENTURY.

NEW ENGLAND INTERIOR 1683. FURNITURE OF JACOBEAN ORIGIN OR TYPE.
Metropolitan Museum of Art.

CHINESE ORNAMENTS OF QUALITY
COMPLEMENT.

MANY STYLES OF DECORATION.

COURTESY H. LEO GOULD, INC.

NEW HAMPSHIRE FARMHOUSE, ABOUT 1720.   (Metropolitan Museum of Art.)

E A R L Y   P I N E   P A N E L L I N G

BEDROOM OF A HOUSE AT SPRINGFIELD, MASS. 1754.
(Museum of the Brooklyn Institute of Arts and Sciences.)

PAINTED PANELS, DUTCH INFLUENCE.
EARLY 18th CENTURY, NEW JERSEY.

Metropolitan Museum of Art.

BEDROOM, CLAREMONT MANOR, SURRY COUNTY, VIRGINIA.

Courtesy William Helburn, Inc.

CHINESE WALLPAPER IN A
PHILADELPHIA ROOM. 1768.

Metropolitan Museum of Art.

PENNSYLVANIA GERMAN DECORATION. 18th AND EARLY 19th CENTURIES.

DUTCH INFLUENCE IN AMERICAN DECORATION.

Photographs from The Metropolitan Museum of Art.

HOUSE OF BENJAMIN HASBROUCK. HIGH FALLS, ULSTER COUNTY, N. Y., 1752.

SCENIC WALLPAPER. A ROOM IN PRESTWOULD, MECKLENBURG COUNTY, VIRGINIA.
ABOUT 1760.

Courtesy William Helburn, Inc.

PAINTED WOOD PANELLING, MARMION, KING GEORGE COUNTY, VIRGINIA.
ABOUT 1750.

Metropolitan Museum of Art.

CHILD'S BEDROOM, ABOUT 1799. HOMEWOOD, BALTIMORE COUNTY, MARYLAND.

Photographs Courtesy William Helburn, Inc.

BEDROOM, CARLYLE HOUSE, ALEXANDRIA, VIRGINIA. ABOUT 1752.

EARLY 19th CENTURY DECORATION IN AMERICA WAS IMPORTANT IN SCALE, ELEGANT IN LINE AND TEXTURE.

Chairs are by Duncan Phyfe; Cornice by McIntyre; Sepia Hand Blocked Paper from France. (Metropolitan Museum of Art.)

LATE 18th CENTURY AMERICAN FURNITURE OF SHERATON INFLUENCE.
Sofa by Duncan Phyfe; New England Hepplewhite Card Tables and Mirrors.

Courtesy Ginsburg and Levy, Inc.

AMERICAN EMPIRE ROOM IN THE
GRACIE MANSION.

Museum of the City of New York.

MUSIC ROOM. ABOUT 1800. HOMEWOOD, BALTIMORE COUNTY, VIRGINIA.
Courtesy William Helburn, Inc.

AMERICAN INTERPRETATIONS OF HEPPLEWHITE AND SHERATON FURNITURE.

Lyre Back Chairs and Table by Duncan Phyfe.   Courtesy Ginsburg and Levy, Inc.

EARLY 19th CENTURY FURNITURE WITH APPROPRIATE WOODWORK AND WALLPAPER.
Katherine Park Studdiford, Decorator.

CHAIRS AND SOFA OF THE FEDERAL PERIOD. (EARLY 19th CENTURY).
Ruth Campbell Bigelow, Decorator.

THE NINETEENTH CENTURY IN AMERICA.

CLASSICISM. -
1800-1840

ROMANTICISM. (Victorian)
1850 - 1880

ECLECTICISM.

1885 - 1900

Photo Ralph Steiner.

HOUSE OF WILLIAM LESCAZE, Architect.

Grey Rubber Tile Floor. Chromium Chairs. Upholstered in Varitoned Corduroy.

Photo Paul J. Woolf.

Eugene Schoen, Architect.

FLEXWOOD WALLS WITH DRAPERY SEPARATING ROOMS.
INDIRECT LIGHTING CONCEALED BY PROJECTING PANEL.

C. COGGESHALL, Designer.
Nyholm Photograph.

CLASSIC DESIGNS FREELY INTERPRETED FOR MODERN USE.

JOSEPH MULLEN, Designer.
Gottscho Photograph.

Photo Richard Garrison.

HOUSE OF MORRIS B. SANDERS, Architect.

CONTRASTING PATTERNS AND TEXTURES BRILLIANTLY HANDLED.

Felix Augenfeld, Designer.

LIVING ROOM BY WILLIAM MUSCHENHEIM.

GILBERT ROHDE, Designer.

WILLIAM LESCAZE, Architect.

PAUL BRY, Designer.

CALVERT COGGESHALL, Designer.
Nyholm Photo.

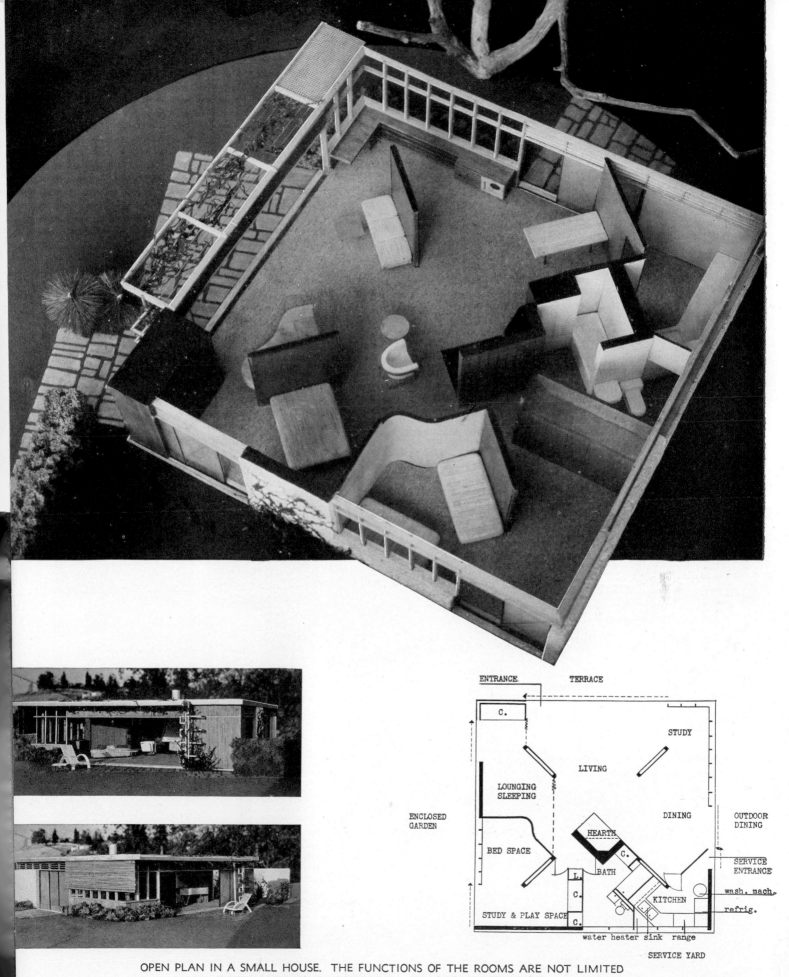

OPEN PLAN IN A SMALL HOUSE. THE FUNCTIONS OF THE ROOMS ARE NOT LIMITED WITHIN THE USUAL FOUR-WALL SEPARATIONS OF SPACE.

Joseph Allen Stein, Architect.

Courtesy Architectural Forum.

Photo Nyholm.

DESIGNED BY ROBERT HELLER.

Photo Rittase.

Photo Kurt Schelling.   Courtesy Arts and Decoration.

PINE PANELLING WITH RECESSED BOOKCASES.

The Wood Tones are enhanced by a Sealing-wax Red Leather Chair, A Blue Green Chair,
A Raisin Carpet and a Parchment Ceiling.

Roy Barley, Decorator.

Bassett & Vollum.

DECORATIVE PAPERS.

Paul Macalister, Designer. Courtesy Sigfrid Lonegren.

Courtesy Kent-Costikyan.

DINING ROOM BY MISS SHOTTER, INC., Decorator.

SCENIC WALL PAPERS CREATE
A SENSE OF SPACIOUSNESS

DINING ROOM BY EMMA HOPKINS, Decorator.

Photo Mattie Edwards Hewitt.

WALL PAPER PANEL OF ACTIVE PATTERN FRAMED IN BY STRONG ARCHITECTURAL FEATURES
Margery Sill Wickware, Decorator.

PAINTED OVERDOOR FEATURE DISTINGUISHES PLAIN PAINTED WALL.
Mrs. Edna Kern, Decorator.

to replace that destroyed during the Civil War. Grinling Gibbons carved and designed superior woodwork. Furniture legs were spiral-turned; chairs had caned and upholstered backs. The three-part oval gateleg tables were popular. During the reign of James II, about 40,000 French craftsmen and their families migrated to England, which further increased the use of French models in England. The crown carved in the deep Flemish style is a typical decoration of the period, standing for the Restoration.

The French Louis XIV could say, *"L'etat, c'est moi"* —but no English king could say this. Though Charles I relied on Inigo Jones, and Horace Walpole said of him that he was England's one contribution to the arts —queer that he never heard of William Shakespeare and so many more!—even Walpole had to admit, "Vitruvius drew up his grammar, Palladio showed him his practice." The Renaissance was merely Europe going to school to interpreted Greek remains seen largely through Roman eyes. Maturity comes after school days. England refused to become un-English for another century, in spite of Renaissance ornamentation on English solidity. The oak of England is fundamentally Gothic. Of all Gothic furniture it is most readily translated into forms suitable for today's use.

X·Stretcher

The Baroque, an exaggerated development of the Renaissance, flowed over Europe all thru the 17th century. It distorted, exaggerated and ornamented the purer early Renaissance form. As an expression of a capricious maturity it evolved all degrees of beauty. The Renaissance came to England as Baroque; it was

Jacobean Bench

applied to the Gothic directly, in a rich but highly refined form. This English Baroque has little in common with that of the Continent or with the pure classic Early Renaissance.

CHAPTER VII

ENGLAND: THE AGE OF WALNUT

WILLIAM AND MARY

The Restoration Stuarts, in their endeavor to imitate the absolution of the French Bourbon monarchs, proved unpopular with the English people, and in 1688 the Stuarts were dismissed, and the Dutch William of Orange and his English wife Mary took the throne. Here was a homeloving royal couple, and mistresses went out of fashion. The royal furniture was Dutch in the main; and Dutch was largely Spanish modified by northern European characteristics. Walnut came in as the principal wood, replacing oak, as had long been the continental fashion. The burning of Whitehall palace gave the new monarchs the chance to introduce a new style that the destructive Civil War had given the Restoration Charles II; and England began to adopt the new Dutch styles with more enthusiasm than they had showed for any styles since the Tudor of Bluff King Hal. The regal and architectural gave way to the domestic. Queen Mary excelled in needle work, and she and her court ladies spent their time decorating, rather than adding to the amorous chronicles of the period.

This domestic quality is responsible for the intimate, livable, human scale of English rooms that make them so plausibly the prototype of rooms today. The use of rooms as we know it is closer to this English example than to any other. The question of light and warmth, the services of the various articles of furniture, were developed from the standpoint of comfort. Ceilings were lower, furniture more usable, and specifically planned for such uses as we now require of it. Colors were warm and subdued.

The furniture was comparatively graceful, slender, and of a lighter style than had previously characterized English furniture. The lines were predominantly rectangular, with the use of both curved and straight lines. The general use of upholstery gave comfort; and, as the craftsmen were predominantly Dutch or French, these influences affected most of the designs popular during the period. The Dutch were great explorers and colonizers, and were laying the basis for an empire whose remains still exists in the Dutch East Indies, Dutch Guiana, Curaçao, and elsewhere. They brought in Chinese, East Indian, and other exotic Oriental motifs, including a profuse use of lacquers and inlays. On chairs and sofas, carving was the chief decoration —and walnut was ideal for this; while on cabinets and tables marquetry and veneers were preferred.

Chair stretchers became flat and serpentine, wandering diagonally from the legs to meet in the center. In tables and chests the stretchers wavered from leg to leg, and often contained a continuation of the inlay work. The Queen began to collect Chinese bric-a-brac of porcelain, and open cupboards became the style, at times glassed in. These cupboards were hooded, as were chairs and settees. The Dutch cabriole leg came in, a more pronounced and shortened thicker *S*. Chair

Grinling
Gibbons
Carving

backs lacked curves, retaining the late Jacobean or Restoration rigidity; and seats were usually square. Grinling Gibbons was the outstanding carver, and carving, as well as paint and lacquer, were constantly employed. Silver furniture, elaborately engraved and carved, came into popularity. A duller marquetry than the late Jacobean was fashionable, graceful curves replacing the excessive decoration of the preceding period. The pendent catkins of the *Garrya eliptica,* a small evergreen shrub, became the favored motif for carvings on chairs and stretchers. In addition to walnut, pear, lime and sycamore other soft woods were widely employed.

Drake foot. Shell on Knee.

Toward the end of the 17th century—William and Mary ceasing to reign in 1702—Elizabethan nobility of line and proportion vanished, before the vagaries of the popular Italian artists, Lorenzo Bernini and Francesco Borromini. These designs came through France and Flanders into England, and, after modification in the direction of quiet domesticity, were generally adopted. Daybeds had become popular during the Restoration; they continued so, with more domestic usage. Bedsteads were increasingly canopied with hangings of velvet and other rich stuffs; and often the French plumes ornamented the corners, or were used with elaborate testers of upholstered and grotesquely carved magnificance; and upholstered chairs began to match them in magnificence, with gilt woodwork as well as the brilliant velvets. The higher nobility went to unbelievable extremes in decorated upholstery as this reign drew toward its close: for national prosperity found expression in simplified utility with more

Table leg. with Claw. and. ball foot. and Lion head

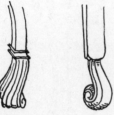

FLEMISH FOOT

SPANISH FOOT

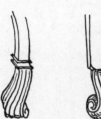

SNAKE FOOT

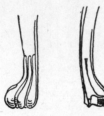

RIBBED FOOT

expensive and valuable materials. Gibbons sought to introduce Renaissance caryatids into his furniture, with small success in English eyes. Mirrors, of every description and decoration, became popular. And everywhere Oriental lacquer in the all-vital cabinets—furniture-makers are still called cabinet-makers in England —and marquetry to match.

QUEEN ANNE

The styles of late William and Mary, Queen Anne (1702-1714) and the early Georgian that succeeded interlock as fully as do the Bourbon styles of Louis XIV, XV and XVI, and the Empire that succeeded. In general, the style brought in by William and Mary continued, with minor changes, until the appearance of Chippendale. Furniture consisted of European designs and decorations, "Englished" by native artists or by the demands of English patrons. The English mode predominated over the foreign importations, throughout most of England, during all these periods.

Anne was the second daughter of the Stuart king, James II, married to Prince George of Denmark, opening the way to the Hanoverian succession of the nearest Protestant relatives of the English royalty. The queen was pious, devout and earned the title of "Good Queen Anne."

Room architecture continued the domestic precedent The mantel became lower and the woodwork became white. The furniture during her reign was curved, with a slight use of straight lines, softened by rounded corners. Walnut was used almost exclusively. The front legs of chairs, settees, stools, tables and other legged furniture were carved; carving stopped with these. The cabriole leg became dominant, with a bolder curved contour, no stretchers, and the club, claw-and-ball, or shell foot. The Dutch influences persisted in marquetry, and in the Dutch duck, pad, club, web, bun, hoof and paw foot. The furniture was lighter, slightly higher, and more rectangular. The backs of the chairs and splats (central panels or supports) in fiddle shapes, spooned comfortably to fit the body. Backs of the seats were considerably narrower than the fronts. Cane backs disappeared during this period. Sir Christopher Wren, staunch friend of the Queen, and Grinling Gibbons are known as the designers of much decorative work of the period.

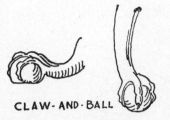

CLAW-AND-BALL

The cabriole leg is traced back to Egypt and especially China, the claw-and-ball foot representing the three-toed claw of the Chinese dragon holding the mystic Buddhistic jewel. Lacquering reached its height about 1710, and was popular for a long period. In addition to walnut, they employed oak, pine, lime, ash and other woods. Love seats, tallboys, card-tables and teatables were especially noteworthy.

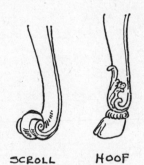

SCROLL HOOF

The double chest of drawers was especially popular. Bedsteads still included the carved oak beds of Norman-Gothic construction, and the decorated tapestried beds rose to unbelievable height and impressiveness, either with plumes or classic designs on the four corners. The bed had became the most important article of household furniture, as in France; and ladies up to the queen gave audience in bed, though men had ceased to.

And now the ages of oak and walnut drew to a close,

Chippendale - Straight legs.

and England was ready for the four Georges, and a use of alien mahogany which gave to the world the shapeliest furniture England has yet contributed, under four master craftsmen and many minor ones.

CHAPTER VIII

ENGLAND: THE AGE OF MAHOGANY

EARLY GEORGIAN

Georgian is the general term for a century of English culture. The four Georges hovered in the background while England grew to dominance. Merchants and soldiers, diplomats and colonists spread the boundaries of Old England, imported and exported and amalgamated cultures.

When phlegmatic George I was called over from Hanover to rule England, in 1714, with his two plump German mistresses and his ignorance of the land and its speech and customs that he was called upon to rule, he did not at first disturb the furniture, highboys, lowboys, and all the rest of the age of walnut. The furniture continued English, with admixtures of French and Flemish design stemming out of Italian Rococo or Baroque.

The choice of a beverage influenced the movement in English furniture styles. Three principal drinks had come into vogue during the reign of Charles I; coffee, chocolate, and tea. Since the empire failed to include the lands furnishing coffee and chocolate, and did control India, China, and other tea-furnishing countries, the Englishman's cup of tea became the custom; and out of this stemmed a furniture to match, including

137

tea tables, tea stands, dumb waiters, and even chairs designed for the tea hour.

Mahogany had been admired by Elizabeth; but its introduction came differently. It was brought to England as a substitute for Jesuit bark, Peruvian bark or cinchona bark, from which quinine was extracted, as a fever cure; and many treatises were written on its virtues in medicine. When his brother brought a shipment of more than one Dr. Gibbons could ever use for medicine, experimentally he decided to use some of the planks in a house he was building in King Street, Covent Garden. Carpenters found the wood too hard, and it was laid aside rejected. When Mrs. Gibbons desired a candle box, Dr. Gibbons told his cabinet-maker, Wollaston, to try the strange wood. Wollaston reported that his tools could not work it. "Get stronger tools, then," said the designer; and the result was the most exquisite candle box ever seen. A bureau was made next; the Duchess of Buckingham begged the remainder of the wood and had furniture made for herself from it; and a new fashion in furniture had come in.

The Georges remained clumsily on at the top of the English social scale, not demanding to rule, quite content to reign; and English independence thrived amazingly during the period. The furniture was a continuation of Queen Anne, but heavier and solider. Castors began to be regularly used on chair and table feet—casters was the original spelling; and this distinguished the furniture from that of the preceding reign. The eagle's head, beak turned outward, was introduced on the arms of chairs. And, while mahogany was the new rage, the conservatives still clung to their walnut.

This was a period of popular rather than royal taste. The Hanoverian German king seemed unconcerned about art; and, with no court leadership in this direction, French and other continental models lost favor, in deference to revived Britishisms. Architects designed furniture to fit their houses, and this gave added heaviness to the pieces, with a reversion to architectural motifs, as if a piece of furniture were merely a replica of the structure that housed it. Scagliola, an imitation stone of powdered gypsum and glue ornamented with such substances as marble dust, took the place of marble, and at times was laid on gilded mahogany bases. The claw-and-ball, the hoof, and the paw foot still dominated on legged furniture.

It was an epoch of architecture. No gentleman's education was complete without a glib knowledge of its language. For a gentleman the Grand Tour inevitably followed the university, and on this European junket the young Englishman acquired the habit of appraising and enjoying foreign cultures. Roman architecture was borrowed for the fronts of bookcases, cabinets, and dressers, even to superimposed columns or pilasters surmounted with entablatures and pediments. The open splat, decorated by narrow vertical cuts, became popular in chair backs. The lion and satyr mask became a distinguishing motif in decoration, appearing even on the knees of cabriole legs. Satyr's heads were often carved in the midst of honeysuckles, with no lese majesty to the Hanoverian sovereign and his mistresses. Winged satyrs were sometimes used. The cabochon—imitating a polished convex jewel—and leaf designs were also used on the knees of cabriole legs. After

Horace Walpole's *Castle of Otranto*, Strawberry Hill, Twickenham, was done over in Gothic in 1747 for the knighted novelist, Walpole sought to reproduce Gothic dilapidation rather than Gothic majesty; so that the production of apparently authentic ruins became the chief effort of architect, gardener and cabinet-maker, as long as this brief craze lasted.

Walpole's paper to imitate stucco was paralleled by others who used plaster and hangings and wall paper and carpet to conceal defects of construction—a custom that may be found in many modern real estate developments. Towers that no one could climb, turrets with no entrance, battlements not worth defending, replaced the inappropriate classic orders; Gothic designs and stretchers reappeared briefly, and vanished. Furniture was upholstered in mohair, silk, velvet, tapestry, and other fine fabrics, and, indeed, these were used to decorate a whole room. Blue rooms, red rooms, and the like became popular, and it was no unusual thing to see vast rooms and halls "papered" with damask and satin.

CHIPPENDALE

In 1727, Thomas Chippendale was brought by his father, a cabinet-maker of much repute in Worcester, to London, where he established himself in Conduit Street, Long Acre. Twenty-six years later, the son removed to Number 60 St. Martin's Lane, where this and three other houses constituted his factory until his death three years after the signing of the Declaration of Independence. The year after he moved, he published *The Gentleman and Cabinet-Maker's Direc-*

tor, with 160 engraved plates—the most important collection of furniture designs so far issued in England. The burning down of his workshops the year following did not harm his popularity, nor stop the continued plundering of his designs by a host of imitators. Chippendale designed and made, or made after the designs of Robert Adam, what his patrons demanded, whether it might be Gothic, Chinese, or the lascive style of Louis XV. He did not introduce the Chinese style into England; he did the best he could with it, as any good workman would. He has left pieces which combine all three styles. These may some day be forgotten, as may even his famous ribbon-back chair, but we shall always remember the balanced solidity of his work.

Chippendale was a magnificent advertiser, and his name was attached to any moment's fad in furniture. He borrowed liberally and added distinction to all he borrowed; with reason he was the most famous of all English cabinet-makers. His chairs, with parts and legs from all sources, are his most successful pieces; his settees were equally famous, and were merely doubled chairs. Some of his most graceful carving was lavished upon the four-poster bed which replaced the horrendous draped sleeping mausoleums of previous styles. He was equally at home in intricate organ case and simple washstand; and though he was grotesque, extravagant or even puerile in many pieces, his level was astonishingly high. He was an artist as well as a man of business, and he gave his name to the greatest period of English furniture, as Louis XIV had to a distinctive French style. We may forget James Gibb's classic vases, the ornate architectural designs of the

CHIPPENDALE
BEDS

chimney sweeper turned architect Isaac Ware, the pier glasses of Batty and Thomas Langley, the mantels and staircases of Abraham Swan, the opulent Chinese ornamentation of Edwards and Darley, the console tables of Thomas Johnson, the decorations of Ince and Mayhew, Robert Mainwaring, and W. and J. Halfpenny; but we will never forget the uneven magnificence of Chippendale's work.

It is common to distinguish between motifs of the English Chippendale, French Chippendale, Chinese Chippendale and Gothic Chippendale, although indeed the motifs are often so intermingled as to be indistinguishable. Cupboards, secretaries, settees, bureaus and dressing tables were more commonly made in his English mode, unless his patron insisted on one of the others; bedsteads as a rule followed his French style; tables were predominantly Gothic or Chinese; and chairs were constructed in all of the modes. Chippendale chairs were constructed primarily for comfort, the seats being square cornered, the size sufficiently large, the tilt tapering toward the back, the upholstery adequate. The uprights at the back flared outward as a rule, a novelty much admired. Walpole, the premier, had removed the duty on mahogany in 1733; and, since mahogany was ideal for carving, and Chippendale excelled in this, it became his preferred ornamentation. He did not use inlay or marquetry, and rarely used turning. The French polishing method was used, of a rag covered with linseed oil with shellac and gum arabic on a layer of cloth around this, which was rubbed on the surface of the wood with a circular motion until the pores had been filled and a brilliant lustre obtained.

The precise chronology of the Chippendale styles, except for contrary demands of his patrons, is as follows:

1735. French influence dominant.
1745. More floral devices; early Chinese influence.
1750. Chinese style predominant. A lighter touch and more French decoration.
1760. Gothic designs, with extravagant design and decoration.

CHIPPENDALE GOTHIC

"THE FRENCH MANNER"

Grace and well-proportioned design marked all the products of Chippendale and his son and namesake, who carried on the business. In addition to his chairs, Chippendale specialized in the "love seats" or "Darby and Joan seats," which were really double chairs with arms only on the two outsides. The French called these sofas *confidantes*. The typical dining table design was two central pieces with wide flaps on either side, and two semi-circular end pieces, all four joined by brass clips. Four cabriole legs supported the larger pieces, and two legs the smaller ones. Mahogany was always his preferred wood. In addition to the pieces mentioned, other noteworthy Chippendale effects were achieved in basin stands, brackets, candle stands, intricate mantel and chimney pieces, china cases, china shelves, clock cases, fire screens, frets, girandoles, lanterns, pier glasses, shaving tables, tea kettle stands.

Through Chippendale's work there is an air of structural design, of permanent solidity. Though he used profusely the most Rococo decoration, it is generally architecturally restrained by strong structural lines.

"IN THE CHINESE TASTE"

The furniture of Chippendale was distinctly *furniture*: the architectural backgrounds were the works of other men and can be more easily classified as Georgian. The fluctuations in style favored the combinations of ornamental forms from all sources.

Chippendale died in 1779. He lived to see the mahogany age, whose leading exponent he was, pass into a more fragile and equally exotic age, the age of satinwood.

Chippendale Mirror.

CHAPTER IX

ENGLAND: THE AGE OF SATINWOOD

THE ADAM BROTHERS

Two years after Thomas Chippendale's workshop burned down, the English at Plassy established the foundations of their empire in India. Four years before the century ended, they took Ceylon from the abject Dutch. And mahogany, the American wood, went out of favor, and satinwood, a beautiful light-colored hardwood with a silky luster, from India and Ceylon, took its place. In furniture it was used for inlays and small veneers, for small articles of turnery, for panels with painted medallions and floral scrolls and borders. It was a feminine wood, for an age grown softer.

In 1748 excavations at Herculaneum and Pompeii were crudely commenced, to be continued for a century. About 1754 a young English architect, Robert Adam, second and most famous of four brothers in business as architects together—the others being John, James and William—visited Italy, and returned with the accurate measurements and drawings of the one Roman private palace he could locate—the palace of Diocletian at Spalato, in Dalmatia. In 1762 Robert Adam was appointed architect to the king, George III. He resigned in favor of his brother James six years later, to erect the famous Adelphi block of buildings on Thames bank. He was the most distinguished archi-

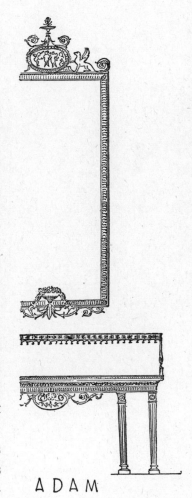

ADAM

145

tect in England, and English style continued his following of Greek and Roman classicism. To him, furniture
was an essential part of the architect's trade: and, to
make his ensemble complete, he expended his genius
on dog-kennels as amply as on royal palaces.

His influence was important on furniture, especially
in the direction of subordinating the importance of
carving. Following French styles, painted furniture
and exquisite inlay work marked much of his work,
with lavish use of the wreath, honeysuckle, and the fan
as motifs. He did not overlook the smallest detail in
designing a room, so that a complete Adam drawing-
room is as typical as a Louis XVI salon. In cabinet-
making, the brothers were designers merely, letting
Chippendale, Hepplewhite and others do the actual
manufacturing of the furniture. They were most at
home in pieces permitting architectural treatment, such
as bookcases, cabinets, and sideboards. They gave espe-
cial popularity to the console table, the classic note
always evident. They did not turn their backs all at
once on mahogany, but slowly introduced satinwood
even for entire pieces, as well as in inlays with holly,
ebony, tulip and similar tropical and subtropical woods.
Cheaper pine and lime woods were used where entire
panels were to be painted. Natural sycamore was often
employed; at times it was dyed gray, and known as
harewood. No classic designs were omitted in the ornamentation, and plaques depicting classical subjects
were often used for decorative purposes.

Painting and relief in the Pompeian manner ornamented all large surfaces whether furniture walls or
ceilings. The execution of these designs by Angelica

Kauffman and her husband Antonio Zucchi, Cipriani, Pergolesi and others was under the Adam direction and purer than the contemporary Louis XVI adaptations. Mantels, doorways and all architectural features that came under their influence were exceedingly delicate.

Thus the classic influence entered England as quietly as it did France under Louis XVI, and no such vast upheaval shook the land as the rise to dominance of Napoleon in the land across the channel.

HEPPLEWHITE

George Hepplewhite was almost a contemporary of Chippendale's, dying only seven years later. Practically nothing is known of his life, except that he carried on business in the parish of St. Giles, Cripplegate. Two years after his death, his *The Cabinet-Maker and Upholsterer's Guide* appeared, with ten designs in another book appearing the same year. With this, the personal record is complete. The name Hepplewhite represents a style rather than one man's own handiwork—a style lighter, and with more delicate grace than Chippendale.

Like Chippendale, Hepplewhite lavished much of his genius upon the all-important chair. He was the great popularizer of the shield back, used in many forms. His chair legs were plainer than those of his predecessors, fluted or reeded, tapering to a spade foot which at times thinned down to the "spider-leg." The backs of these chairs were often adorned with festoons of wheat-ears or pointed fern leaves, or with decorative use of the Prince of Wales's feathers. The general effect of these chairs was of extreme fragility. The

HEPPLEWHITE

painted and japanned satinwood pieces lacked decorative permanence entirely; with little use, the paint wore off, and had to be renewed.

Hepplewhite was also noted for his window-seats designed for the tall, narrow Georgian sash windows, and for countless smaller pieces: urn-shaped knife-boxes in mahogany and satinwood; inlaid tea caddies; delicate little fire-screens; painted work tables; inlaid stands. At times the work shows the height of elegance and a delicious simplicity; on other pieces it sags to unimaginative commonplaces, or virtual ugliness. Among his tables were drop-leaf ones with one square and one oval end, two such tables being formed together to form a longer one. During this time occurred the decline of the highboy and the lowboy, in favor of the wardrobes and chests of drawers similar to modern chiffoniers. The classic note continued through all of his furniture, being taken both from Louis XVI styles and the designs of the Adam brothers. One unusual addition to furniture design was the Duchess chair or tete-a-tete, consisting of two joined armchairs, one faced reverse from the other.

Where carving was a part of his design, he clung to mahogany; but satinwood, sycamore for fancy veneering, white holly for inlay and division lines, and others more unfamiliar were used by him. On his satinwood panels appeared the decorative paintings of Angelica Kauffman, Michael Angelo Pergolesi, and other Italian artists. Sideboards and desks were decorated with carved rosettes, festoons and medallions, employed with chaste restraint. For upholstery, horsehair stuffing came in, covered with satins, silks and other fine fabrics.

Even the pillars supporting the testers of his beds were slender, although there was a use of ornate Oriental domes to crown many of the draperies.

SHERATON

Thomas Sheraton, like Hepplewhite, followed the styles of the Adams but leaned more toward the Louis XVI and later French sources. We hear of him first in London in 1790, when he was about forty, though he may have migrated much earlier. In spite of his work, which raised him second only to Chippendale in critical eyes as a cabinet-maker, he never emerged above a poverty almost sordid. He designed more than he did the actual work, and eked out his scanty living by giving drawing lessons, and writing. Sheraton's *The Cabinet-Maker and Upholsterer's Drawing Book,* issued in 1791 and twice reprinted, dismissed Chippendale arrogantly as wholly antiquated, and found nothing to praise in any previous book on the subject. In his designs, although he was sometimes original, he was also a successful adapter, and on occasion a mere copyist.

His later style tended to the tortured and bizarre, as the popular demand for French Empire drove him beyond the extravagances of the French. Chairs had backs of fabulous animals, with "knees" and legs made of the heads and claws of crowned beasts. His delicate and harmonious lightness was replaced by squatness and heaviness. He devised many "harlequin" or disguised pieces of furniture so popular in the late 18th century, such as a library table concealing a stepladder to reach to the top rows of bookcases, a dressing-table concealing a washstand and escritoire, a looking-glass enclosing a dressing-case, a writing-table or a work-table. He even devised an ottoman with "heating urns" beneath, to keep the seat warm in cold weather—long anticipating streetcar, bus and train heated seats. He at least anticipated the ugly hall chair of mahogany, with the owner's crest painted on the back, which was popular long after our Civil War. His genius was less sane and balanced than that of Chippendale. When he yielded to the Empire style, he rioted in sphinxes and lions and fabled monsters, in dull and cumbersome forms, in massive and uninspired brass mounts, and led to the decay of English cabinet-making, which brought in the uninspired period of Victorian Revivalism.

It is better to remember him by the grace of his earlier pieces. For all the excessive slenderness of these, they were soundly constructed, and have outlasted many heavier articles of similar type. His upholstery differed from Hepplewhite's, in that he revealed the frame, instead of entirely concealing it. His chairbacks were plain, lyred, or urned, the top line straight or slightly broken. Slender fluted legs, round or square, tapered down to natural or spade feet. Chair arms were straight, or continuously curved from back to front. Caning marked many of his pieces. Instead of the serpentine front of Hepplewhite's sideboards, Sheraton preferred a complete convex or a single swelling, set between square ends. He often used the brass railing at the back introduced by the Adam brothers, and concealed in the interior all sorts of small drawers, shelves and boxes. Countless kidney-shaped desks and tables, card tables, sectional bookcases, and wardrobes complete the distinctive Sheraton contributions. Satinwood was his favorite material, with mahogany for chairs, and for veneering. Carving was rarely used—chiefly smaller Adam forms, such as rosettes, urns, sunbursts and vases. Ivory and brass key plates and metal drawer pulls were of the utmost simplicity. In inlay, he has never been surpassed, using kingwood, zebrawood, tulip, rosewood, and holly as his chief materials, often divided by narrow lines of ebony.

OTHER GEORGIAN DESIGNERS AND CRAFTSMEN

The same astonishing Georgian period also produced Robert Manwaring, Thomas Shearer, William Ince and Thomas Mayhew, Robert and Richard Gillow, Mathias Lock and Copeland, and others of great ability as designers and cabinet-makers. Manwaring was in the mode, but designed more heavily than the others. Shearer was the equal of Sheraton and Hepplewhite in dainty simplicity. He gave the sideboard its characteristic modern shape, as distinguished from a mere sideboard-table with drawers. He influenced both Hepplewhite and Sheraton.

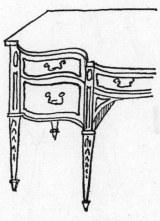

SHEARER

Ince and Mayhew were most noted for chairs. The Gillows were more famous for workmanship than for design. Richard Gillow invented the first billiard table; and in 1800 he invented and patented the telescopic dining table, one of furniture's most useful inventions. Lock and Copeland followed the tradition of Adam religiously and effectively.

CHAPTER X

THE NINETEENTH CENTURY

ENGLAND: THE REGENCY

It is hard to understand the poverty of design of nineteenth century England. Even those great designers who carried over past 1800 showed the most startling coarsening of their styles. It may have been the loss of the French inspiration, perhaps the changes in social groupings, or the new spirit introduced by the machine and new processes. Whatever the cause, our perspective of the 1800's shows England rich and increasingly powerful, expanding in the sciences and in social concepts and with virtually nothing in the arts.

The French Directory and Empire were cheerfully absorbed by the contemporary English, bitter as their political hatred may have been. The Empire style became a great wave of Greek and Roman inspiration with Thomas Hope succeeding Sheraton in the Classical pattern. The Regency period in which George IV was regent for his father had a furniture of a more comfortable, domesticated Empire feeling, usually in rosewood or mahogany, or black and gilt paint. Against plain walls, papered or painted with lively, solid colors the effect was one of material solidity. Architectural designs were a heavier classic, rather severe with broad pilasters: deep, flat cornices; flat arches over doorways,

Thomas Hope
English Empire niches and recesses; floors were carpeted, except in

152

public rooms, which had black and white marble squares. Fabrics were used lavishly in great and often over-elaborated draperies. They tended to plain or small patterned silks, satins and damasks, with stripes, geometrical and classic motives.

VICTORIA

Victoria ascended to the throne in 1837. England was still classic, but without enthusiasm. A revived interest in Gothic came and went, influencing monumental architecture more than furniture. Sir Walter Scott was partly responsible but was not alone. Later Ruskin and William Morris cried the virtues of the style from the roof tops. To the English people it was just so much archeology, and satisfied no deep need. Neither, however, did any other style offered, new or old. The result in decoration was mixture and modification, to such a degree that the productions were neither good copying, interpretation nor originality. Style became styles. Fashions on the continent attained the voluptuous coarseness of the Second Empire and England likewise adopted squat, writhing lines for chairs and tables and sofas.

Sir Charles Eastlake epitomized the period through the seventies by publishing a book of designs for furniture based on the medieval. The current factory-made output was based on his well-meaning ineptitudes. The result was machine lines with bits of ornament, metal and tile panels and grooves and turnings.

Infinitely more important is William Morris, 1834-1896, though as an impulse rather than a creator of style. The aesthetic weakness of the time was apparent to many people, but the self-conscious styles they offered were no improvement. The Pre-Raphaelites strove toward a return to Gothic directness. Morris, Burne-Jones, Rossetti, Ruskin and others designed every kind of decoration, furniture, textiles, stained-glass, wall papers, printing types and books; they wrote poetry and painted and established the lines of a cottage style of architecture. Corollary to their handwork idea was their Arts and Crafts movement which spread over Europe and America. For the last fifty years English architecture and decoration has been indelibly influenced by this thought. Morris was imbued with his conception of the merits of the medieval age. His idea of house decoration favored return to hand work, to the massive simplicity of oak furniture, or the delicate beauty of inlays of choice woods and the charm of painted furniture. He favored considering the material, object, method and purpose of a work as essential conditions of its artistic expression, the form and character of which must always be controlled by such conditions. This was at least an attempt to frame a workable philosophy of furniture and decorations. One of his inventions achieved enduring popularity because of its comfortable utility—the Morris chair, simple in design, with adjustable back, and removable cushions in the seat and back. It may have been in use before Morris's time, but he gave it its popularity and its name.

However, except for a few manifestations of genuine artistic thought and conception like this, this was the period of Eclecticism, or choose-your-own style, in which fantastic machine-made products and extremist cabinet-maker designs alternated with period revivals.

Mankind was fumbling. People who had little taste were influenced by the selling pressure of merchants or manufacturers. People of genuine taste found little of value in the original creations of the period and so had to select from the creations of previous periods so that the distinguishing feature of this Eclectic period is that there was no distinguishing feature.

GERMANY

Our investigation of historical decoration has been restricted to a few countries not arbitrarily but because each of these—Italy, Spain, France and England—developed an individual climax not parallel to any other. Styles grew concurrently all over Europe, but in the main their growth and climaxes followed those of one of the lands considered. It is interesting to make a side trip to Germany to consider a unique development which has recently been a source of interest.

Germany, like the rest of Europe, followed the Paris styles through the Renaissance, Baroque and Classic revivals. After Napoleon, the German and Austrian styles took over the Empire, like the rest of Europe, but in modifying it to their materials and conditions developed a plump, straightforward classicism. It was provincial, with a naïvely architectural detail; it utilized the native woods; cherry and pearwood and beech, with black, brown and gold trimming; it replaced the imperialistic symbols with domesticated flora and fauna. It tamed the martial spirit and made it placid and amiable.

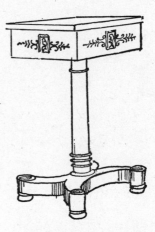

BIEDERMEIER

Papa Biedermeier, circa 1830, was as familiar to the readers of *Fliegende Blätter,* a German humorous weekly, as Mickey Mouse is to today's movie devotees. His good-natured thickness, his *gemütlichkeit* became in later years the symbol of things old fashioned, solid, a bit ludicrous. The name stayed on to signify this furniture and its stolidity. The German designers of the time probably thought they were designing in the French style; the fact that they made good solid Empire beds of light cherrywood or painted pieces that they could not execute in fine woods did not change their feeling about it.

These local interpretations are always a source of interest to the furniture archeologist, revealing as they do the process of communication and interchange of ideas, and the effects of local variations. The Empire versions of Sweden, the Flemish and Dutch Renaissance, the classic styles of Russia, were all highly distinctive interpretations.

CHAPTER XI

EARLY AMERICAN

American Colonial is anything but a consistent style. Each colony was settled by wholly distinctive types of people. They were recruited from differing social classes and they left their homes for various reasons. They landed in climates ranging from sub-arctic to sub-tropical, and they maintained varying degrees of contact with the home country, but very little with each other. It is therefore not remarkable that on the American continent we have echoes of Yorkshire yeomanry in New England, Georgian elegance in Philadelphia; aristocratic French in Charleston, and medieval German in rural Pennsylvania. Further south we run into the French and Spanish influences, the Spanish concentrating in Florida and the extreme west coast, and the French developing the Mississippi bayous and the Gulf section. The consequence of all this is that the different sections produced distinctive architectures and types of furniture. While they are commonly lumped as Early American or Colonial, we must use discretion in combining them, even though their dates are identical.

The customary separation of Early American styles is into three periods:

1. Early Colonial, the era of settlement up to 1725.

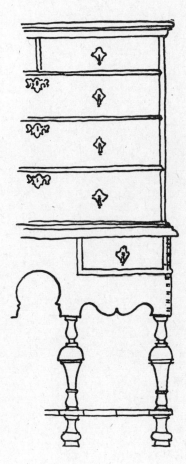

Highboy —
Trumpet Turning

2. Late Colonial, the period of consolidation of importation and development up to 1790.

3. The Federal period, 1790-1825.

In Virginia in 1607, in Plymouth in 1620, in Massachusetts Bay in 1630, in the other colonies later on, clear down to Georgia in 1733, the same conditions roughly applied. Settlers had been disembarked from a ship, at best with only a minimum of furniture, and at times with none. Their food supply could last only for a limited time. Simultaneously they had to clear the forest to provide gardens and fields for cultivation, room for a house, and timber and lumber for a house and its sparse furnishings. They were quite happy to live without furniture at first, since they had at least a roof over their heads. Among the settlers in each colony were some better skilled at carpentry than others: and these took over the work of knocking together rude crude articles of furniture from remembered English patterns where the individual colonists were incapable.

The earliest style might be called a colonial imitation or reproduction of English cottage furniture, in the main. It could hardly be called Jacobean, or any other name applied to court furniture down to the age of Chippendale. It was the provincial style, chiefly survivals of Romanesque Norman and Gothic, with such later additions to Tudor and Elizabethan or Jacobean as had come from seeing court furniture, or from hand-me-down pieces presented to the yeomanry by the nobility, when they turned to new pieces or a new style. The English colonists did not have to invent their furniture; but they did have to reduce it to the utmost simplicity and utility, and to learn to utilize native woods. Clearing the forests, cultivating the stubborn soil, guarding against hostile Indians, fighting off sickness, accident, starvation—these left little time for elaborate furniture-making. Moreover, the custom in peasant homes—and many of the settlers came from little better—was the minimum of furniture, and that all for utility and nothing for show; and there was no disposition on the part of the first settlers to expend energy turning their homes into a Nonesuch Castle or a Versailles.

NEW ENGLAND

The New England colonies had a religious motive. The Mayflower voyagers and their immediate followers brought over very few pieces of furniture, and it is very unlikely that for some years after they landed they devoted much of their precious time to the making of decorative fripperies, even had their religious concepts permitted it.

Their houses and their furniture were therefore of the simplest. Houses began as single room shelters, with the dominant enormous fireplace reminiscent of the English yeoman's cottage, without the decoration. A central chimney probably was an early improvement; this tended to divide the house into rooms, and the specialized uses that followed undoubtedly gave each of these an individual appearance. For economy of material and heat, ceilings were low and windows small; the beams were left bare. Some small decorative effort was spent on chamfering and slight moulding, with red and black touches on the raw wood.

The early wall finish of wattles was soon displaced by plaster, or wood panelling. The recollection of the wood surfacing of rooms in English homes plus the ease of working the noble pine, gave the Puritans the opportunity to rationalize the use of fine wall panelling.

The first furniture was of the same crudeness. Since the Pilgrims came chiefly from provincial stock, the articles they may have brought with them were certainly not in the current advanced fashion of England. In 1620 the English Gothic was still the important form of design in the Provinces, and such furniture as travelled to America or was made here for many years was Gothic. Chests were carved with motifs out of the 16th century English, using oak or pine. Stools and chairs were patterned after the turner's work of the Jacobean countryside. They made trestle tables, hutch tables and gateleg tables, with legs turned and often trumpet shaped. Chests began to develop as rapidly and thoroughly as in Europe. By 1680, the Gothic quality had disappeared and everything was simplified with no cost to its design or utility. Ornament as such was rare, but the ornamental spirit crept in exquisitely in the treatment of home made iron implements such as latches, fire tools and kitchen utensils.

The first quarter of the Seventeenth Century saw the extension of colonies throughout New England, with varying degrees of restriction on the accumulation or the display of wealth. These new settlers inevitably brought expansion ideas from Europe and the other colonies. The death of Cromwell ended the Puritan influence in English furniture, and the Puritan furniture of America after 1660 echoed Charles II and William and Mary in provincial versions. While the characteristic gilding and inlaying never touched here, New England did produce highboys and lowboys and chairs and tables with clear Restoration and Dutch features. Other appurtenances of good living came over: mirrors and fabrics particularly: chintzes and other imported fabrics appear on the lists, as well as articles of silver. The English Windsor chair came over and was transformed into a triumph of American design. American Windsor chairs from 1700 to 1800 give evidence of an underlying sense of good structural principles, fine feeling for the material employed and real skill of handicraft. These came to replace the stiff ladderback and are the symbol of greater comfort and better workmanship.

Between 1680 and 1725, New England houses began to display a change in economic state. There were more rooms: the living room was no longer the kitchen; panelling was painted white and more furniture was in use: cupboards, chests and dressers. There was a variety of fabrics, mostly imported, as were many of the pewter and silver articles.

NEW YORK AND THE DUTCH

The Dutch settlers along the Hudson established themselves after 1624 as farmers and landholders. They built solid low stone houses, with typical gambrel roof, constantly referred to today as Dutch Colonial. There was little architectural pretense about these rooms, and the furniture was as direct and serviceable as that of the New England colonists. The Kas was a storage chest derived from the Armoire; surviving examples are brightly painted. The English, who captured New Amsterdam, changed its name to New York and endeavoured to make it thoroughly English. The difference was that it was a gentlemen-merchant class that came here, not the religious enthusiast of New England. Accordingly furniture was more worldly and came principally from Old England for many years.

Some Dutch settlers moved into Pennsylvania, where they met similar migrations of Swiss and German colonists. This group is now identified as the Pennsylvania Dutch. Their household furniture is still reminiscent of 17th century Europe, a peasant art distinguished by quaint decoration in color.

THE SOUTH

Virginia, the Carolinas and Georgia emerged from the pioneer state very early in the sixteen hundreds. The settlers had originally been drawn from Cavalier and Royalist classes, especially during the Commonwealth, and were added to by younger sons and gentleman-adventurers. By 1700, there was in these states a distinct aristocratic tradition. The climate and the introduction of slavery made possible tremendous plantations; they produced wealth and a leisure class which followed closely the current styles of the home country. From Charles II on there was a definite predilection for French styles in the Southern colonies, exactly as there was in England.

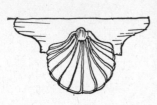

The plantation house developed quickly into an Italian-English form better adapted to its climate than the prototype in England. High large rooms with large windows characterized these houses at an early date, and the fine standard of daily life fostered the importation of the best types of English furniture and their

reproduction. The treatment of rooms followed closely
on the English and there are in Maryland and Virginia,
Carolina and Georgia many rooms of the early 1700's
that are purely Georgian in decoration.

This development seeped slowly northward through
trade. Philadelphia, New York and Newport came under the spell of this opulent style. Local cabinet makers everywhere now followed the English imports. The
style of interior architecture in all the colonies reached
a fairly coherent level by the time of the Revolution.
Active commerce with the West Indies, Holland,
France, England and Africa (including smuggling,
rum and slave trading) created a wealthy class of merchants in New England and the North. These built spacious homes and furnished them richly. Walnut and
mahogany panelling in the classic spirit decorated the
living room that ran the length or the width of the
house: ship's carpenters were often called upon to do
this decorating. Styles from overseas were indiscriminately mixed up in an early eclectic fashion, and this
constituted the height of New England smartness.

The Revolution caused a recoil from everything
English, in favor of everything French, Spanish and
Dutch. This meant primarily Louis XVI. But the
cabinet-makers were trained in the styles of Chippendale, Hepplewhite, and Sheraton, and thus the Georgian styles, slightly modified in the direction of simplicity, continued to be used by the ex-Colonials. Tea
tables, "pie crust" tables, highboys covered with Oriental lacquer, and cabriole chairs were especially popular. At this time William Savery, a Philadelphia
joiner or cabinet-maker, created some distinctive styles

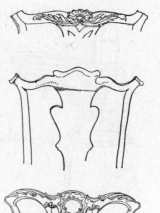

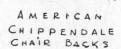

AMERICAN
CHIPPENDALE
CHAIR BACKS

—a crossing of Chippendale and the softer feminine lines of Louis XV. Black walnut was used at first, though by 1770 mahogany had come in, to replace the fine walnut growing along the banks of the Schuylkill! Curly maple was the preferred substitute for satinwood. The more excessive European decorations, painting, marquetry, and inlay, never became popular in the colonies.

By the time that national independence had been won, America might have been regarded as ready to initiate its own style in furniture. But for decades yet America continued provincial to Europe. It felt no necessity to express its sense of arrogant independence in a new style of furniture and decoration. When its first own style arrived, it was a mere reflection of European conditions.

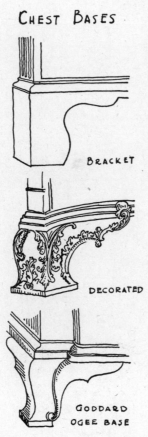

CHEST BASES

BRACKET

DECORATED

GODDARD
OGEE BASE

CHAPTER XII

THE FEDERAL PERIOD AND AFTER

The Revolution is a convenient dividing line for the American style. While the national sentiment was inflamed against the British, French themes were resorted to directly; as it subsided the ingrained habit of looking to England came to the fore. Only politically did the ex-colonists exist as non-Englishmen. Besides, English styles at this time were so French that it hardly mattered. The elegance and delicacy of Louis XVI and the directory merged with the influence of the Adams, Sheraton and Hepplewhite.

Duncan Phyfe is the prophet of this period. Born in Scotland and having learned cabinet making in Albany, we find him in New York about 1795. From this year until about 1820, he produced exquisite furniture in the tradition of Adam and Sheraton, using mahogany almost exclusively, with very particular selection as to the quality of the wood and the technique of construction. He catered to the well established upper class, commanded handsome prices, and made good furniture which survives in museums and collections.

From 1820 on, the Empire influence grows more and more pronounced in Phyfe's work. We cannot say whether the interpretations were bad or that Phyfe was no stronger than a bad style, but it is certain that the master designer was faced with the alternative of losing his mastery or his customers.

165

Finial with Eagle.

AMERICAN EMPIRE.

By 1830 his work had reached the stage of being designated by himself "Butcher furniture"—ponderous, graceless bulks in rosewood. Of course, by the time Phyfe died, in 1854, the standard of taste everywhere had been debased by all the complexities of the machine influence, by an enlarged smugness into which we do not look too closely for decorative inspiration.

Two New England architects, Charles Bulfinch and Samuel McIntire, closely followed the Adam style, rendered more simple and austere. Thomas Jefferson went directly to the classic sources, as befitting a true democrat, and designed buildings and rooms that were purer than the French or English Empire forms.

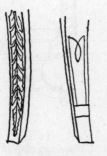

Curved feet

AMERICAN EMPIRE AND LATER AMERICAN STYLES

Rooms of the early 1800's, as seen in the preservations in most of the large cities on the seaboard, generally show fine proportions and fair size, the walls invariably treated with architectural distinction, the details of window trim and mantels, cornices and doors, and built-in cupboards all inspired by a noble architectural conception, elegance and restraint dominating. French themes are present throughout, especially in the gracious forms of crystal chandeliers, fine fabrics, and highly decorative mirrors. Yet the whole feeling is that of the English manner of the Adams. In the more provincial centers the same themes carried through wood panelling and some wall paper; maple in the characteristic mahogany forms; and reproduction as near as possible of the grand manner offered by the examples of the large cities.

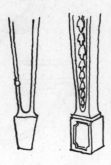

Square feet

The persistence of the Empire style is only partly

responsible for the Greek revival which assumed a leadership in the 30's. Of course the local carpenters that indulged in the outbursts of Greek temples for Congregationalist churches, had more architectural precedent for exteriors than interiors. As a result the interiors of some of these Greek temples were an assembly of motifs hanging over from the earlier Empire, crossed with a variety of classic forms imported from England, France and Germany.

Empire furniture had in America a better development and a longer life than in England. The sofa was a significant piece with curving ends whose flaring legs terminated in carved feet depicting the lion's paw or the eagle's claw—the borrowed Hittite eagle being the American bird, but the lion being still predominantly British. At the top, a straight top rail turned back, terminated by carved eagle head ends. Bedsteads were of the gondola, sleigh or four poster type, the "pineapple beds" having their four posts terminated with pineapple designs. Posts in a bed had been designed to support tapestry. Now the tapestry was gone; but the meaningless posts persisted. Nothing breaks up the lines of a room more than meaningless posts jutting up in the air, even when joined by cross bars: it is as if a large room had unnecessary small pillars scattered here and there to decrease its roominess. But the custom persisted for a long time.

Tables had drop leaves, or leaves to be inserted, usually with square ends. The support was usually a massive plinth or pedestal in the center, with flaring legs which ended in lion's feet. Sideboards went classically architectural, with scroll or pillar supports, two end

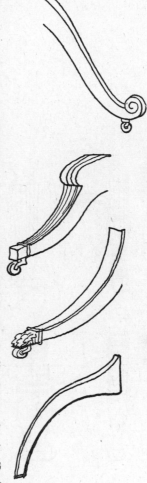

Table Feet

doors and two central doors. Soon a looking glass was invariably set in the back rail, often with shelves above it. Mahogany was the preferred wood, with symmetrically matched veneers placed on pine; though curly maple and even rosewood were at times used for extra elegance. As woodworking machinery came in, carving disappeared. Drawer pulls were of glass, or brass rings set in lion's mouths. Caned settees were often painted black, with gold stripes. The mahogany at first was polished to a brilliant lustre. Later it was dyed a deeper, richer red.

The German Biedermeier had an indubitable effect on the painting of furniture, the dark coloring of walls —in fact the treatment of the entire interior.

Then there was a neo-Grecque style—stubby, solid supports, a general air of thickness and self consciousness epitomized in the early Currier and Ives prints —The Soldier's Return and other Mexican war gems of sentiment.

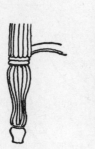

There must have been in New York hundreds of rooms with dark blue walls and cold white highly architecturalized mantels and doorways, in which the furniture included a Recamier type of sofa, a very architectural table, and some low-back, rather Greek side chairs, great festooned draperies of satin or silk, with ponderous fringes and gilt architectural cornices.

The Clipper ships brought over objects which introduced an alien motif and were cheerfully imposed on the classic base—China gods and lacquer work, silks and screens mingled cheerfully with the cold austerity of these classicisms.

Turned Feet.

There was also a Gothic influence during the 40's

and 50's, and many lesser houses and cottages of this time show this development. It is possible that Sir Walter Scott renewed an interest in medievalism which was reflected in the jagged work that festooned itself along the gables of some of the houses in this country, and gave the country carpenter with a busy jigsaw such a magnificent opportunity to sell something. Tables and chairs were not overlooked in the deluge of lacy appendages that were tacked on to rather pure structural designs. Jigsawing with turning represents the introduction of machine design into American furniture—about 1840. Machine turnings made possible production in inconceivable quantities of the spool turning, which could be assembled into beds and chairs without restraint. These wiggly lines disported themselves over acres of 1850 rooms.

This effort to stuff machine processes into furniture, coupled with very little esthetic discernment, is responsible for the reign of terror in design that followed for the next fifty years.

The Victorian influence came principally from England, and we know it as the Black Walnut and Horsehair Period, and the interior architecture of the time was a ponderous brown-tasting motley. Belter in New York made Victorian Louis XV shapes of Rosewood.

The Eastlake was translated into oak and plush in the eighties. In the nineties, a great self-consciousness broke out after the Chicago Fair; the architects urged a return to classicism—Imperial Rome and the Beaux Arts in buildings, Louis XIV and the other magnificences in decoration. Another stream favored the Empire revival, while a decided swing toward the Arts

CHAIR BY
BELTER

and Crafts of William Morris found a native style in the Spanish Missions of California. Architecturally, the nineteenth century ended without having found itself.

CHAPTER XIII

THE TWENTIETH CENTURY

The twentieth century opened so hopefully! It was hailed as the dawn of a new day, a better mankind. Actually it was a changing world, destined, in the United States particularly, to have a new face before its first quarter had passed. Architecture, communication, the material world simply changed its style; it didn't evolve at all. Architects tried for years to make tall steel buildings reminiscent of stone ones. As the scale increased they made overhanging cornices so large that legislation alone could intervene to save our sunlight. At first, automobiles were made in the image of carriages; early ones were known to have whip sockets. It took some years to let an automobile look like an automobile. The airplane had nothing to start with so it became a thing of beauty in its own right.

Decoration has not been so fortunate. The first quarter had a cycle of experiment with unhappy results, after which we fell back for security on the old fundamentals. In the last twenty years, good traditional style in furniture and decorations has been available to everyone. It does not detract one bit from the intrinsic beauty of these styles to say that throughout this span of years, we did not create one distinctive thing that compares, as a symbol of our time, with the airplane, the motor car or the construction of our buildings.

171

The early years of the century were groping with a fine mixture of rugged individualisms. The European designers were in a state of hysterical rebellion against their stale classicism. The Art Nouveau in France, the Jugendstil and the Secession in Germany, Craftsman or Arts and Crafts in England, and a similar movement in Austria . . . these were all objecting to something and what they produced was rebellious, self-conscious, arty. With the slower European pace, however, they kept at it. Art education in Europe has fairly consistently been along lines of principles, not archeology or research.

In this country, however, we grasped at every straw. As each wave of Arts and Crafts, Art Nouveau and what-not came over, the furniture manufacturers picked out their obvious features and incorporated them in their lines for that year. We know the results: Art Nouveau became bird's-eye maple, cherry-red-mahogany and twisted silver. Arts and Crafts came back as Mission—clumsy oak blocks, hammered copper and burnt leather. There was a deliberately amateur quality about all these, which excluded studied forms and the subtleties of fine perceptions.

Our perceptions as a people were increasing during this period. Contact with Europe through the war and post-war era made us aware of the superior artistic attainments of the older nations. Each chose the style he liked best and built or rebuilt his home along that line. Of course, since the elements were the furniture, dealers in antiques recognized and encouraged the American market. The taste being established, American manufacturers had nothing to do but follow. Those buyers that could afford them, purchased antiques; others acquired copies.

The sad part of this approach is that it has become a matter of fashion. One year's style is Spanish, the next year there is a movement to popularize German Baroque; the following season we fall back on Empire. This factor of style will either drive us into a form of temporary stage settings, or an avoidance of all fashion out of sheer economic necessity.

We have, however, come to recognize that a certain homogeneity of style is desirable. A street of mixed houses, white Colonial next to stucco Spanish, half timbered English or Peasant Norman, is an architectural museum. A procession of styled rooms in house or apartment may be just as unconvincing, as shallow. If, as individuals or as a people, we really want to express ourselves it will follow that there will be a certain consistency to our background. It follows that while we may use as fragments all the styles in individual pieces, the background will evolve out of the building's character and requirements.

CHAPTER XIV

CONTEMPORARY DESIGN

Mark Twain's Adam, in the Garden of Eden, was astonished by Eve's readiness in naming the animals. Our use of Modern as a word to label the current approach to design will be just as anomalous to a later critic. Its ultimate name will come when another set of people can get off on a hilltop and see us as a whole. Until then it is not for us to quibble between Modern, Modernist, or Modernistic. To some individuals, Modernistic damns the output of the 1928-29 period; it is not unlikely that these critics will be compelled to invent some similar vituperation for our present creations.

Axiomatically, this new method of designing has no rules. Any style begins with a few individuals working in a purely personal way. Their influences spread, coalesce and develop. When faced with similar problems their results are almost identical. Yet the variety of their character, attitude or vision is bound to be noticed. Most phases of the modern styles up to 1935 were distinguishable as personal interpretations. After that date the various movements became larger than the individual, more comprehensive in the variety of output, even though inspired by the same individual sources. This process of outgrowing the individual reveals the magnitude of the movement.

Our first attempts at modern design were importations of these personal methods of European designers.

These began in an appreciable way after 1925. That year the French Government invited the various nations to exhibit at the International Exposition of Modern Decorative and Industrial Arts at Paris. It was stipulated that the exhibited material must be original and national in character. It was something of a shock to ourselves to realize that while Europe thought of us as the dynamic inventors of a new civilization, we had in furniture nothing but second hand copies of what the French and English and Italians had achieved in previous and different civilizations. Instead of an exhibit we sent a commission which discovered that Europe was not working along the same lines that were occupying us; that they were doing things that they thought expressed their time; that as realists they knew that every generation has its own impulses. Within two years the cosmopolitan cities of America were swimming in a whirlpool of Modernism. Every major department store had an exhibition of Modern Decoration as a matter of fashion necessity. The Ile de France steamed into New York in 1927, a glittering boatload of Modernism. It was all accepted as it came and lumped together as modernism, praised and ridiculed. The copyists went to work. Without analyzing the individual rightness of each solution, the whole was borrowed, shaken together and served up. The flavor was singularly like some of those amateur early prohibition cocktails.

Not immediately apparent nor generally understood was the fact that there were then—and still are—two distinct schools, each thinking of itself as new and modern, yet basically farther apart from each other than either was from the recognized historical styles. Broadly characterized, one school might be labelled the Romantic or Decorative School; its antithesis lies in the Functional or Architectural approach.

The first school views contemporary decoration as a revaluation of historical decorative styles in terms of current tastes, materials and social expressions. It seeks to paraphrase, to revise the idiom, but to express the same fundamentals. It is evolutionary; there is a clear line of descent from the pictorial four-wall quality of the great historical periods, from the Art Nouveau of 1900 and the Viennese Secession. Its primary reason for being is change, merely change; the healthy human cycle of novelty, enthusiasm for fresh individualisms, the love of variety and kaleidoscopic brightness that is inherent in young and gay people. It is *fashion,* rather than *style.* As such it encourages exploitation by the makers and sellers of things; it makes for rapid change, quick turnover, the speedy obsolescence of merchandise. It is constantly on the alert for unexploited basic styles; thus we have had the succession of Classic Modern, Chinese Modern, Swedish Modern, Modern Baroque, etc., etc. It is a commercial age, and the commerce in design is stimulated by speeding up the wheels of fashion.

The roots of this style are European but its exploitation and development are purely American.

Europe was closer to America in the 1920's than at any other time, and its unpedantic, freehand methods of using design forms struck Americans as utterly new. The fact that in those years most European designers had merely picked up the ravelled ends of 1914 mattered not at all. Most of the exhibits in the 1925 Paris Exposition were clearly evolved from work familiar throughout Europe for many years. The style was emotional, suave and ornamental; in some cases it attained great beauty and elegance. It employed flowing lines, ivory and metal inlays on exotic woods, precious materials, and exquisite handicraft. Some of it was imposed on graceful Directoire and Classic forms; more grew out of the uninterrupted tradition of the Art Nouveau, the Viennese Secession, the Jugendstil, the Wiener Werkstatte. The exquisite, cultivated design of Ruhlmann, Leleau, Adnet, Dufrene, and many others in France; Bruno Paul, Peter Behrens, Josef Hoffman in Germany exhibit these evolutionary trends. Fresh and sparkling, possessed of great intrinsic beauty, they graced interiors planned in the traditional way. They changed little in the organization of the room; they were essays in another decorative idiom.

Less commendable were those tendencies inspired directly by the turmoil in art forms of the era. Cubism became a mannerism in furniture design, in the patterns of textiles. Jazz motivated bizarre forms and colors. Grotesquerie and unrest were the characteristic expression of designs fomented by unschooled rebels; there was more rebelliousness than design. Eloquent arguments by powerful egos made much of the tradition that new things are often inhospitably received; also that it is essential that the age express itself clearly (and loudly) by abandoning all that has gone before and improvising its own tune. There was much talk of new materials, as if the machine had just appeared, or as if it were the starting point of design. It was a good vocal art.

It might be said that the 1920's were the years of the birth of design-consciousness in America. Inevitably European-trained designers fathered this birth, and just as inevitably, there were reminders of the parentage. Joseph Urban, Paul Frankl, Winold Reiss, Wolfgang

Hoffman, Frederick Kiesler, Lucien Bernhard, to name only a few, led the way with designs for rooms and furniture, generally clear and straightforward and handled with decorative facility, humor and grace. Their imitators and disciples more often interpreted the letter than the spirit. The personal mannerisms were too often crossed and confused; irrelevant improvisations betrayed the effort, and as a sincere style it failed because the motive was unsound.

Reaction grew from two roots. One was a movement toward oversimplification, the complete abandonment of decorative effort. This root was the Functional movement, or the International style, whose abstractions in form were illogically detached from the background, misunderstood and misused to the point of destroying its validity. The other root of reaction was in the historical styles, in paraphrases of which—"modernizations"—designers hoped to evoke an aesthetic crystallization of the era, as the Brothers Adam had evaluated the grandeur of Rome into 18th century London. Reasonably, the simplest shapes were most adaptable, and the early 1930's made much of the classical adaptations. Source material from Egypt, Greece and Rome, as well as the traditional modified classicisms of the 17th, 18th and 19th centuries, inspired a considerable school. To some extent this constitutes a current of Stylism intermittently felt in varying intensity in the style market.

One of the most successful phases of this movement has been the Swedish Modern. Classic origins are only faintly apparent through the common sense shapes and colors, agreeable softness of contour and texture. Proportions are small, comfortable and familiar; light woods, muted values of clear colors, and a general air of reasonableness have made it a distinct, popular style for several years.

In another direction, the influx of emigré designers from Germany and Central Europe has established a considerable trend toward the playful forms once identified as Viennese. These have light proportions, suavely moving outlines, and imaginative, fanciful play of surface and color. Graceful lines and refined scale give this work a luxurious, somewhat feminine quality, still not reminscent of any of the historical styles.

Again, the limitlessness of the Baroque styles has inspired a free scale in some of the more pretentious decoration. It cannot be said that there is a definite expression of Baroque furniture, but rooms planned by some outstanding designers reveal a new breadth of scale, the free use of great sweeping curves, a lush palette and extravagant textures. Furniture is eclectically chosen to emphasize or to offset these qualities; some has sinuous lines resembling the 17th century Italian work, other pieces are severely rectangular. Rather novel features are apt to characterize such designs, as the use of extraordinary materials, unusual proportions, or striking dramatic compositions. The range of this manner is necessarily limited to those few virtuosi who can handle it with knowledge as well as assurance; in lesser hands it may be vulgar and showy.

Strangely enough, the lesser part of modern design is based on simple rational forms, unstyled and free of snob appeal. To the extent that such work has a sound background in unstylized architecture, it may truly be the basis of our style.

Viewed as style, most of the categories mentioned above lack the basic impulse to a new style: a new beginning in Architecture. Until very recently our construction system, a new thing, tried to make itself look like the old. Few people questioned the propriety of distorting the dimensions of a Medici Palace to fit an apartment building. Strangely, this was regarded as proper and good architectural design, while the architect who made no attempt to disguise the steel-and-concrete body of his building was considered affected. Similarly, the decoration of the rooms was predicated on an arbitrary choice of old furniture, and the background—the vital anatomy of the house—was masked with a harmonizing stage-setting. Hence the affectation of interior architecture.

When "modern" was selected as the "decorative" period the same effort was required to make a harmonizing background. In this light all style, when deliberately effected, is reduced to an expression of fashion, a mannerism. If, however, the background or space delimiting factors are directly structural, the need for decoration is nothing but a matter of agreeable and practical compositions, utilizing the functional or working elements of a room—the furniture—and the decorative features: pictures and sculpture, plants, etc.

It is not in the province of this book to study the development of house types, but we cannot arrive at an understanding of interior design without appraising the form and growth of the shell. The modern house is not distinguishable as a modern house merely because it has a flat roof or glass bricks; it may achieve its modernism with none of these. A modern house is one which assumed its form because the people who occupy it live and move in a certain way and utilize certain facilities and materials. Since some of these factors are new and different it is plausible that a house planned with respect to these factors will look and operate differently from a house built for another set of factors. So viewed, the modern house is a compound of the servant problem and plywood and electricity, bridge and the rumba, the depression and high taxes and nursery schools, glass bricks and radio and rayon and insulating and automobiles, reading in bed, stainless steel, labor problems, transportation, amateur photography, oil burners and ten thousand other ingredients. One of the products of many of these factors is the Open Plan.

Frank Lloyd Wright is indubitably one of the earliest architects to employ the elements of the open plan house. His perception was recognized to the extent that his houses in the Middle West dating from 1940-1910 were widely admired for their picturesque effects, but made no other impression on architects or buildings. But the prophet was not without honor in other countries, and in Japan and in Germany Wright's work was understood and acclaimed; his work abroad came back to America with new connotations during the 1920's. War and the new economy bred some aspects of social change, and in Europe a mature aesthetic sense took account of these factors, plus the various newcomers in material and usage and method. Architects turned away from mere prettiness. Names like LeCorbusier, Gropius, Oud, Van der Rohe, Asplund, are associated with the new concept, the revitalizing of Sullivan's phrase "Form Follows Function." Because electricity and concrete and sunlight are the same everywhere, such designs tend to a broadly universal appearance. Hence the names Functional, International.

The understanding of the new house form is only now becoming widespread. Architects exposed to European influence are spreading the idea, and thoughtful local phases are appearing simultaneously in California, New England, Florida, and the Middle West. These informally organized houses are primarily concerned with better utilization of space, economy of building and operation, comfort and suitability; less with the conformation to a type or pictorial effect. Their interior design is free to follow comfort, usage, unorthodox combinations of elements. Thus, a truly modern house is less concerned about the exact styles of furniture, because there is an inner harmony of structure and its occupants. The scene is complete regardless of whether the chairs are of Biedermeier origin, or of bent tubing; they are only chairs, and the owner may indulge his whims. Actually it appears that most modern houses carry through the clear harmony of simple furniture shapes, probably because people who like that kind of house also like that kind of furniture, if it serves them best with least fuss and most directness.

Simplicity may be accepted as the preeminent feature of this new design, but we need not accept the purely mechanical line as the essence of simplicity. In the welter of advertising and styling clichés the word "functional" has exposed itself to the worst criticism; as if a sharp corner is more functional than a rounded one. In the effort to simplify planes and angles, some designers have forgotten the human frame. Planes can be just as well defined without mechanically sharp edges, but it takes more skill to do it. This skill is becoming more highly developed.

The chill harshness is giving way to a greater congeniality of effect, whether through the softening of the line, the more judicious use of contrasting textures, or a wider vocabulary of forms. And, finally, we are becoming used to it. Seen from another angle, there are objects that appeared outrageous but now begin to express a new beauty through a harmony and directness. The tubular steel chair as an unrecognizable form is disturbing and unpleasant; yet through continued use one is apt to recognize through its basic soundness of construction, its lightness and comfort, a wholly new kind of satisfaction. Against a proper background it will develop a harmony and sincerity that may come to be recognized as just as truthful and fine an expression of its age as the most exquisite Hepplewhite chair is of its own time.

The truthful use of new materials always develops a new understanding of related textures, colors and forms. Just as 18th Century England studied and emphasized fabrics and metals that blended with mahogany, so will we find ourselves organizing a palette around aluminum and plastics, rayon and rubber. If these materials do not lend themselves readily to a given purpose, the mature designer will not attempt to torture them into being what they are not, but will use everything at hand for the furtherance of his mind picture.

Let your first criterion, then, of modern furniture be "Is it natural and reasonable?" This will eliminate the tricky, the gaudy, and the obviously "styled." There can be no such thing as authentic "Modern."

No infant style starting on its career ever had so many materials to draw on or such highly developed technique in using them. Cheap modern furniture is no better nor no worse than cheap period furniture to-day, and the same elements of fine workmanship and a reasonable price must prevail. There are some technical features about the design of modern furniture that, if improperly executed, invite greater expense and uncertainty; and these demands must be accorded their due consideration. To illustrate, the flush surfaces that are accepted as elementary in modern design are not fundamentally good woodwork, as they do not take into account the tendency of various grains of wood to move microscopically. No such flush joint can reasonably be expected to remain exactly as it was made, over a long period of time. Most historic furniture has lived because the nature of the material was taken into account and the design was made accordingly. This is just as true of wood to-day as it was two hundred years ago.

Similarly, anything experimental or new is no more perfect than the old. And the modern as a style or system of design may not be considered entirely free from the likelihood of such failures. Likewise, bizarre exaggerations of any shape will in all likelihood suffer with the passage of years and not contribute on the whole to the formation of a clear and distinct style. The tremendous puffed-out upholstered chairs will not necessarily be more comfortable for their elephantine proportions. Nor can the argument of logic be applied to the solid bases of chests and beds that so quickly become a medley of vacuum cleaner dents. There is an infinity of such details that may be gleaned from the average store display of modern furniture. It is likely that under some particular condition the design may suit admirably, but it seems more likely that as such features constitute a valid objection to the design they will give way to less vulnerable expressions.

Almost no one wants to recreate wholly the setting of a bygone day. The real objection is constantly offered that the most beautiful furniture has already been designed—that we have only to use with tender responsiveness the forms and key-notes given us by a better age. This obvious Chinese ancestor-worship cannot be taken seriously. By this criterion, no poem may be written nor picture painted; the world is full of the fruits of other creative minds. But the same presumptuousness that prompts new poets every day to strum their lyres has its same budding in the effort of every decorator, amateur or professional, to inject a new and personal note into his work; not to accept unqualifiedly that which is offered or that which has been done to perfection. So long as this work has the faintest earmark of an art, it must comport itself as an artistic expression—the irresistible outburst of the individual's ego to make things that look good to him.

To-day we are faced with one of the most virulent of these recurrent human explosions. The surge of a new feeling that roused painting in the middle of the 19th century has its counterpart now in the esthetics of daily living. Whether this has grown logically out of a new architecture that was forced on us by new human demands and new materials to meet them, or whether the architecture in its esthetics is catching up on its mechanical advances and pulling inferior design with it, is beyond the point. The fact remains that for millions of people to-day there is an unsolved dissatisfaction with a purely traditional approach to interior architecture and a hopefulness and willingness to experiment with new forms. It is this variety of forms and approaches that we consider as Modern.

Modern decoration as a style is still in a state where, if you don't like it you can change it. It is not necessary to accept any single feature that is displeasing. Because of its dominant plainness, combining it with highly ornamented period furniture is liable to be unduly conspicuous, but the mixing of styles must be governed in every instance by taste. So far as it is possible to summarize the characteristics of modern decoration and furniture today, they may be listed as follows:

1. A general subordination of the individual pieces of furniture to the form of the whole room. The whole composition is most important.

2. Simplicity of planes and surfaces. No piece of furniture should be difficult to comprehend at first glance.

3. Clean straightforward surfaces. The individual surface should not detract from the composition of the piece or its part in the room.

4. The tendency to lowness rather than height. Space is essential in a room and we can conserve it by not filling it with furniture. Low lines are restful, easy to live with.

5. Woods are left in the most natural state consistent with proper preservation, omitting staining, graining and excessive polishing.

6. Acceptance of the possibilities of textures, for contrast and harmony and the interplay of varying textures of fabrics, metals, woods and other substances.

7. Avoidance of grotesque shapes, trickiness, gadgets and stunts. If the excuse for doing the thing is a special purpose, it must serve that purpose better than anything heretofore designed.

8. Whatever the function, the ornamental or decorative aspect must not interfere or hinder.

9. The pieces of furniture should be easy to handle and maintain.

PART II

THE ELEMENTS OF DECORATION

CHAPTER XV

MATERIALS OF DECORATION

The elements with which the decorator works are:

MASS
LINE
COLOR
TEXTURE

The MASS of the room must be considered as a hollowness—the whole space. This we attempt to make larger or smaller in appearance according to the function and character of the room. The MASS of objects within the room must be studied with relation to the MASS of the room.

LINE is the moving element in contrast to the immovable mass. Line may define a mass, accent it, or cut it up.

COLOR is that element of surface which may be used either as mass or line. In a flat picture it is both; in solid, three dimensional things, color may be used or omitted for emphasis or otherwise.

TEXTURE is the feel of material.

Colors in a room are associated to have a positive effect on each other; textures offer just as effective a means. Textures have been mostly considered through fabrics but textures are walls and woods and metals and glass—all the materials that we use—the surface quality. You can make a room composition with textures. A room may have every object the same color and still have the widest range of feeling, because the various textures will throw off or swallow up light in such different ways that they produce different color feelings.

In a single room, one might take the some color to calcimine the ceiling, paper the wall, carpet the floor, use wood of the same color, leather, wool, silk, rayon and cotton; and yet the sharp contrasts in texture might keep it from being monotonous. Each material has a different touch. This quality is one that the eye can distinguish. Texture is like timbre in music. A C-sharp on the piano, violin, and oboe all played together will produce one note, and yet each is distinct and the combination is more beautiful than the individual note.

Woods are given different finishes in order to emphasize texture—open grain, closed grain, high polishes and dull. Metals are given brushed or satin finishes or are highly polished. Glass may be ground or may be bought with one surface figured, prismed, dotted or etched, for the sake of texture. Materials may well be of entirely one color, yet varying effects or patterns will be introduced in texture by means of self patterns, ribs, weaves, etc.

Highly polished textures tend to be elegant and formal. Rough textures—tweeds, open-grain woods, hammered iron, shaggy uncertainly figured carpets, rough plastered walls, have an association of open air and country life. Damasks and highly polished wood and ormulu inlays suggest the delicate, the French.

The actual materials with which the decorator achieves his ends are unlimited. They are the materials used in furniture, woods, metals and upholstery materials; the fabrics of curtains, carpets and rugs; glass and wallpaper, stone, linoleum, plaster, rubber, leather, and the synthetic materials.

FURNITURE WOODS

Since wood is the primary material for furniture, we should begin a study of its essentials with some education on the subject of woods themselves: first the technical nature of woods; second, the classification of woods; and third, the methods of using them.

Wood has been and is at present the most desirable furniture material for many reasons.

1. It is readily available.
2. It is easy to cut and shape.
3. It is easily joined together with nails, screws and glue.
4. It is beautiful in itself, with great variety.
5. It is comparatively light in weight.
6. It does not conduct heat readily, therefore is neither too hot nor too cold at the touch.
7. It is not noisy.
8. It may be repaired easily.

On the other hand, we must remember always that wood is an organic, natural material, extremely uneven, unreliable, and subject to unpredictable behavior and eccentricities. In endeavoring to overcome these characteristics, the manufacturer goes to the source to determine the causes and endeavors in the very beginning to cut or cure wood to avoid or lessen the danger of this misbehavior.

Wood is composed of long fibres between which sap is transported from roots to leaves. This is possible because of the ability of the wood to absorb the sap or moisture. However, there is a disadvantage in this continued absorption. Wood is cut so as to get the most continuous fibres with the length of the board and to utilize all the stronger part of the tree. (The bark, of course, is useless as timber.) Long after the wood has been cut, it continues to have the capacity of absorbing and throwing off moisture, according to the atmosphere in which it stands, and from this spring all the evils of warping and splitting, checking and twisting.

The different sections of the tree when cut into boards produce different effects; and it is these various grains that give rise to the wide number of possible patterns that we employ in decorative furniture. The trunk of the tree, for instance, is the long grain, and in most trees this exhibits a pronouncedly striped effect, more or less fine. The section toward the root where the trunk fibres swing out and produce a cross section we call butt. This will usually have a sort of crinkly texture, in addition to the long grain. The crotch, from which the limbs and branches develop, always produces a highly figured V grain of extremely decorative character, usually accompanied by a tendency to crack. There are certain cancerous growths called burls that occur on trees, which when removed and sliced, yield burl veneers, highly figured, usually pitted textures which have very effective natural designs.

There is much confusion as to soft woods and hard woods, which isn't cleared up by the fact that botanists classify them one way and lumbermen another. To the

STATELY MODERN USE OF CLASSIC DERIVATIONS.
ROBSJOHN - GIBBINGS.

Richard Garrison Photo.

Photo F. S. Lincoln.

A NOTABLE WOOD FLOOR IN A FRENCH CHATEAU.

Octagonal Mahogany Panelled Room by Jacob (Period of Louis XVI). Chateau De Méréville.

Sara Hunter Kelly, Decorator.

Van Anda Photo.

HOUSE OF ALMOS EVANS, Architect.

Drix Duryea Photo.

SCREEN PANEL OF RIBBED GLASS.

Joseph Aronson, Designer.

AN IMPORTANT DOORWAY YIELDS A VISTA
WHICH IS ENLARGED BY THE REFLECTIONS
IN A LARGE MIRROR.

Harrie T. Lindeberg, Architect.
Photo Gottscho. Courtesy Arts and Decoration.

CAUCASIAN RUG. 19th CENTURY.

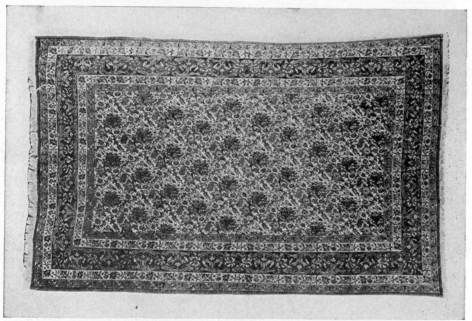

PERSIAN RUG. 19th CENTURY.
Victorian Flower Pattern

TURKISH RUG. LATE 18th CENTURY.
Photographs Courtesy McMillan, Inc.

THE BEAUTY OF THE HOME AND SWEET MUSIC ARE SYⁿ

DECORATIVE TREATMENT OVER A SMALL STAIRWAY
WHITE WALLS AND DEEP BLUE CEILING, ENLIVENED BY
BRONZE STATUETTES AND A PAINTED INSCRIPTION.

Alexander H. Girard, Architect.

AN IMPORTANT SCULPTURE SET UPON AN ADEQUATE BASE.
The arrangement of the Sofa, etc. opposes the absolute symmetry of the Bookcase Wall.

Alexander H. Girard, Architect.

TOMMI PARZINGER
Designer.

Lee Coyne Photo.

DECORATIVE USE OF LEATHER.

FELIX AUGENFELD
Designer.

Brammer Photo.

ARCHITECTURAL TREATMENT OF LIGHTING.
Virginia Connor, Designer.
Gottscho Photo.

JAMES F. EPPENSTEIN, Architect.

Hedrich - Blessing.

William Lescaze, Architect.

Costain Photo.

WINDOW TREATMENT.
Designed by Margery Sill Wickware, Decorator

DINING ROOM.

By Miss Gheen, Inc.

Gottscho.

FOYER IN A SOUTHERN HOUSE.

Paul MacAlister, Designer.

Photo Harold Costair

NEW ENGLAND CLASSIC DOORWAY FRAMES A SERENELY BALANCED GROUPING.
Verna Cook Solomonsky, Architect.   Lucille Schlimme, Decorator.

HARWELL HAMILTON HARRIS, Architect.   Dapprich Photo. Courtesy Architectural Forum.

LIVING IN SMALL SPACE DEVELOPS NEW AND INGENIOUS COMPOSITIONS.
Above—A disappearing Dressing Table in a Clothes Chest of White Holly.
William Muschenheim, Architect.

BOOK ALCOVE IN LIVING ROOM.

Evans Moore & Woodbridge, Architects.   Van Anda Photo.

Ethel A. Reeve.

DECORATION SUBORDINATE TO DOMINANT
ARCHITECTURAL FORMS.

Margery Sill Wickware.

Margery Sill Wickware.

SCALE AND BALANCE.

Robsjohn - Gibbings.

LIVING ROOM IN A COUNTRY HOUSE. Howe and Lescaze, Architects.

"A ROOM WITH A VIEW" MAY BE DRAMATIZED BY MAKING THE WINDOW
THE FRAME FOR THE PICTURE. VENETIAN BLINDS ASSIST BY MODIFYING THE
LIGHT WITHOUT SACRIFICING AIR OR PRIVACY.

Design by Sylvia Holt, Decorator.

PAUL LASZLO, Designer.   Fred R. Dapprich Photo.

PAUL MAC ALISTER, Designer.

HAROLD SCHWARTZ, Designer.
Richard Garrison Photo.

C. COGGESHALL   Nyholm

Drix Duryea

COMBINATION ROOMS—JOSEPH ARONSON

F. S. Lincoln

botanist, all deciduous or leaf-shedding trees are hard, and all non-deciduous trees, which retain their leaves all year, are soft. According to the lumberman's classification, some deciduous trees are soft, based on actual physical texture, while some non-deciduous trees like yellow pine are decidedly hard.

After the tree is cut, the problem of seasoning arises. Air drying is the first step, and as the boards leave the sawmill, they are stacked so that the four sides will be exposed to air. There are certain minima for each kind of wood, varying from about three months for the white wood family to as much as ten or twelve years for some of the tropical woods. Practically all wood is kiln dried after air drying. It is put into a sealed chamber in which the temperature is raised gradually so that the moisture is carried off until this warm air has taken up all but a desired percentage of the dampness from the wood. This must be done very slowly in order to avoid the too rapid loss of moisture which would produce cracking; some of the tropical woods take six or eight weeks in the kiln even after years of air drying. As a general rule in this climate the average native wood is left with about 5% of the moisture. Then the wood must be stored properly so that it is not unevenly exposed, or subjected to dry heat or conditions that do not represent a good average climatic exposure.

Through all this, wood remains an organic material. Few people can predict just what results it will give. Most manufacturers, as far as their choice goes, use well dried, well seasoned wood because it does not pay not to. The fact that at times the material acts badly is apt to be due to a faulty design, improper construction or disregard for the nature of the wood itself.

The soils that nourish the trees are usually reflected in the character of the wood. Color, texture, grain, and strength vary according to the chemistry of the soil in which the tree grew.

After the wood is brought into the factory and is ready for use it may be used as a solid lumber or cut into thin layers, as veneers. To many people the word "veneer" is inseparable from the word "cheap"—a thin veneer, in the literary sense. But the special fields of veneer and solid wood do not overlap; there is a structural or decorative need for each. Veneers are slices of wood between $\frac{1}{16}$ and $\frac{1}{20}$ of an inch in thickness cut in cross sections. The slices are therefore fairly identical as to grain, and by matching the slices a repetition of the grain produces a very interesting pattern. Then the veneers are applied to a backing of a material capable of holding them together. Thus we begin to *synthesize* wood.

Just glueing one thin veneer on another thick layer invariably has the effect of causing the wood to bend thin side in, which indicates that there is a greater tensile strength in proportion to the thin wood than to the thick.

Plywood follows. This consists of a thicker semi-porous core, on both sides of which are laminated exactly equal thin veneers $\frac{1}{16}''$ thick or less, with the grains of both veneers running exactly perpendicular to the grains of the core. This is called the cross banding. On top of that is applied finish, the veneer with grains running parallel again with the core. This produces a plaid with all tensions pulling in different ways. Veneers alone have no strength, but this lamination makes them strong.

In former times veneers achieved evil repute because they were inexpertly constructed and the adhesives were poor. To-day the glues themselves are stronger than the woods they hold together. Generally when there is any break, it occurs in the wood and near the joint, and almost never in the glue joint. In plywoods, therefore, we have an almost synthetic material with the beauty of texture, pattern and color of the natural product which has never been duplicated by any process, but with far greater strength and permanence than the solid wood. Recent developments in the field of adhesives have enlarged the scope of plywood enormously. Among the new glues or cements are the phenolic resins, caseins, and the tego process. These aim to produce panels impervious to moisture, bacteria, heat and cold, and to eliminate technical evils such as staining, and open joints in veneering. Use of plywoods in boat hulls, airplane fuselages, and house exteriors, suggests the degree of success that has been attained. To summarize, the virtues of veneer are:

1. It is stronger than the same thickness of solid wood.
2. It cannot split or crack through.
3. It permits the economical use of fine woods.
4. It allows for flat decoration in furniture by arranging the grains of the woods into patterns.
5. It facilitates the use of shaped work other than flat surfaces.

FREQUENTLY USED WOODS

Many fine cabinet woods are produced in the United States, and have a long and successful history in furniture making. We have maple, birch, beech and oak, pine, walnut, poplar, magnolia, holly. Woods differ in weight, adaptability to working, texture, color, strength, also in preciousness or rarity.

Some woods are rarely used other than as veneers, but most of the domestic woods are used principally as solid woods or as the basis for commercial plywood.

AMERICAN WALNUT is really one of the noblest cabinet woods available. It is medium in color and hard enough in texture for the best wearing qualities, but not too hard for the wood-worker to use comfortably. It lends itself to slicing or shaving for veneers, as admirably as for solid use. It has a wide variety of grains and textures which may be permuted at will and practically all of which are ideally workable. The American walnut is a reddish brown. The straight wood has a parallel combed grain, but nearer the heart of the tree this will be more highly figured. The butt of the tree produces very interesting large designs which can be beautifully matched as veneers and which frequently exhibit a cross grain or "cross fire" which enhances its beauty. The walnut crotches are likewise capable of producing very beautiful effects when matched as veneers. The American walnut burls run to very highly figured dark spots of a birdseye character, and likewise are the basis of a great deal of decorative veneering. Walnut is one of the highest priced woods produced in America, and the supply is dwindling due to its great popularity and the failure to replace the growth. Historically, this walnut has been used for much furniture of the style produced in the colonies which are now the Middle Atlantic States, from the middle 17th century to the present day. The Pennsylvania Dutch settlers used it, and, indeed, fine furniture of walnut was produced in all the colonies at all times, before and after the Revolution. Walnut reached its zenith around the Civil War—the black-walnut and horsehair era, in which the wood was twisted and stained into shapes and colors that left a sour taste in the mouths of several succeeding generations. American walnut is admirably adapted to modern furniture because it offers so many types of grains and because, on the whole, it is such a satisfactory wood from the cabinet-maker's point of view.

French walnut has a grayer color, more satiny texture than the American. It was very extensively used in all phases of furniture making.

The walnuts of Spain and Italy are fine textured and with a reddish cast. The great achievements of the 14th, 15th, 16th and 17th centuries in both countries were executed in this wood.

The English walnut reached its apex during the reign of Queen Anne, and the whole school of furniture design of the latter half of the 17th century may be interpreted in this wood. Highly figured burls with marquetry are most characteristic of the time.

One of the most exotic walnuts is that from the Caucasus—the Circassian walnut that had a brief period of over-popularity in this country some twenty-five years ago. The wood is intrinsically beautiful but so dramatic that its use over many large surfaces tends to make it tiresome—which accounts for its fall from fame.

The so-called Australian walnut, which growers deplore as being not a true walnut, is a beautiful wood with a strong striped grain in contrasting blackish brown and lighter brown, an agreeable texture which finishes very similarly to walnut, and which has been quite extensively employed in modern American and English work.

MAPLE is second only to walnut in the native woods. It has come to be identified as a symbol of Early American, although what sometimes passes for a mellow old maple is a little sad. Maple is one of the lightest woods grown; also one of the hardest. It occurs bountifully practically everywhere from the Atlantic to the Mississippi, from Canada to the southern highlands, although it has an infinite variety of textures according to the locale and source. We have very hard rock and sugar maples from Vermont and Michigan, and soft maples from the uplands of West Virginia. The New England colonists found it beautifully adapted to their turnery and the 17th and 18th centuries in New England produced its most characteristic work in maple. Usually it would appear that this wood was left unfinished or perhaps given a light oiling and waxing, to which time added a patina, darkened and mellowed to a variety of shades ranging from a honey tone to a deep molasses color. It certainly under no conditions produced the hot reddish cast that passes to-day for "antique" maple.

Maple is used in its curly form, in which the curly figure is highly parallel; in its straight or run-of-the-mill figure, which has a subdued grain, and in a burl form which is an intense orange brown with beautiful quilted figuring and birdseye. It is used extensively for plywood as well as the solid lumber. Legs of tables and chairs and similar structural members are particularly well made of maple.

The birdseye in a burl is different from the birdseye grain. Practically all the grains of maple are used in modern work, and at the moment a particularly highly favored wood is the bleached white maple—a very delicate blonde tone.

BIRCH grows principally on the northeastern seaboard and in Canada. The best hard birches come from the Adirondacks and Vermont and New Hampshire, as well as Wisconsin and Michigan. Birch has a beautiful, rather wild, grain. It has the strength and the cutting properties of maple, and a great deal of "maple" furniture is birch. Soft birch (white) is not as desirable as the hard birch. It exhibits decided tendencies to split and crack, and as a general rule one rarely finds it in furniture.

BEECH is not popular in this country, although it has decided value for legs of tables and chairs and similar structural parts. On large surfaces it has a tendency to warp and few manufacturers use it. Beech has always been used extensively in France and middle Europe.

OAK is one of our finest woods, but this generation has been unable to overcome the prejudice growing out of the frightful things that were done to it thirty years ago. In itself a beautiful wood, hard and susceptible to a fine finish, it was then stained or varnished to a remarkable ugliness. Oak was used throughout the Colonial and early Republican period, but in a more rustic capacity. We find comparatively little fine furniture in this country made of this wood.

The English furniture of the Tudor and Elizabethan periods represent the greatest achievement in oak. Their finishes varied from a middle tan to a smoky black. The rather finer texture of English oak makes it more acceptable. The wood is very pleasant for wall panelling as there is much vibrancy in its texture.

CHESTNUT has a grain similar to oak, is slightly more brownish and much softer. It is used somewhat for reproductions of English and French furniture, and to some extent for wall panelling. Its principal value to the cabinet-maker is structurally for the cores of veneered sections. It is so porous that it acts as a very sound base for the glueing of the veneers and by permitting the passage of the moisture at will it reduces the danger of warping to a minimum.

ASH is a very hard, very light wood, whose grain resembles oak. The American ash has never become the subject of much furniture making, except for the interior parts of the frames of upholstered furniture, for which it is particularly desirable. The Hungarian and other imported ash are used as veneers with very decorative effects.

ELM likewise has a large grain. The wood is soft and is not well adapted to furniture.

GUMWOOD is very extensively used in this country for furniture and interior trim. In moderate and low priced furniture, some gum is invariably used in structural parts, or in the cores of veneered sections, as it very successfully imitates mahogany or walnut. Gumwood, when properly kiln dried, is quite serviceable, but when improperly handled is most dangerous. When used for solid tops and similar unrestrained sections, it frequently warps and cracks. Under this name of gum-wood there are a number of trees, most of which grow in the southern states. The water gum, or tupelo, is the best adapted, but there are others; the black, cotton and red gum are the commonest trees in the South.

The tendency now is to make fruit trees grow smaller, which of course diminishes their production of lumber. In previous times pear, apple and cherry were very considerably used for furniture. The apple wood and the pear wood are practically eliminated now, but there is a certain amount of cherry wood still available in sizes and quality suitable for furniture work. It is surprising that more is not used, considering its rarity, because it is really a very beautiful wood and excellently adapted to cabinet-making and furniture.

BASSWOOD is used very extensively for the core stock of veneering and panels on account of its porosity; it works easily and is often used also for the inner parts of cabinets and chests, etc. Yellow poplar and magnolia are in the same class.

BUTTERNUT, sometimes called White Walnut, has a very agreeable light brown color, and a grain approximately like that of walnut. The wood itself is not very well adapted to construction purposes, but makes a good veneer.

IMPORTED WOODS

MAHOGANY is, with walnut, at the head of the list of fine furniture woods. It is available in the greatest variety of grains and figures. It can be used for all structural parts as well as for veneering in the widest variety of patterns. No mahogany grows in the United

States, the principal sources being the West Indies, Mexico, Africa, and the northern part of South America.

The wood itself is highly lustrous, generally of a reddish brown color varying from light to dark in shade. Although very easily worked, it is sufficiently hard to resist wear. It shrinks, warps and checks very rarely, and takes a very pleasing finish. Since its importation into England and France at the beginning of the 18th century it has had continuous favor.

For a decade or two in the early 1900's an unfortunate habit developed of staining it either very dark or very red, and giving it a high piano finish. No crueler abuse could have been inflicted on this beautiful wood, because mahogany is neither red nor dark—actually a light orange-brown tone, which has a tendency to become very mellow with age, but definitely not blackish. A crystalline deposit in the pores gives it a sheen which increases with age.

Philippine mahogany is not a true mahogany. The color and apparent texture of the long grain good are similar to true African mahogany, but it is much more fibrous and soft, and not as adaptable to structural uses in the same way as the true mahoganies. The trees are known as Tanguile or Red Lauaan.

LESS FREQUENTLY USED WOODS

ASPEN is an American wood of the poplar family. It has a beautiful light color and silky texture, with light brown stripes. There is a semi-cross fibre in some aspen, particularly in the crotch cut, which makes it extremely decorative. Modern furniture has made extensive use of it.

AVODIRE (an African wood) is a distinctly blonde wood with a fairly indistinct grain, also used considerably in modern work. Both Aspen and Avodire veneer well.

BALUSTRA (South America) is a very dense, hard wood of a light tobacco brown color. It has a distinctly oily texture.

ACACIA varies from light brown to shades of red and green, and has a figured grain.

GONCALO ALVES or BOSSONA, a Brazilian wood, has a decided black and brown streak on a red-brown ground. It is very hard and horny, and sometimes shows a tendency to develop surface cracks.

BOXWOOD: The Boxwoods that come from the West Indies are very dense, light colored and grained, and are used almost entirely for inlays and small decorative articles.

BUBINGA, from Africa, has a beautiful closely striped grain on a red-brown ground. It veneers quite beautifully, takes a very handsome finish, and has deservedly found considerable use in modern work.

COCO WOOD is an Indian product and is very hard and brittle, with purplish brown stripes on a medium dark ground.

WHITE HOLLY is a domestic product. Because it is the whitest and least grained wood available, it has been highly favored in recent modern work.

KOA from Hawaii has a reddish stripe on a yellow-brown ground, with a very decided cross ripple or curl which gives it a brilliant plaid effect. Since it is showy, it can be used for highly decorative effects. It takes a fine lustrous finish when properly rubbed.

LACEWOOD comes from Australia. It has an eccentric brilliantly pock-marked surface which gives it the lacy effect from which it derives its name. It also is used as a decorative veneer in modern work.

LAUREL WOOD (Africa) is a yellowish brown with a texture and grain like a lighter walnut.

MACASSAR EBONY has been highly favored for recent work, particularly in France and Germany. It has an intense black stripe on a reddish brown ground. It is very hard and takes a brilliant polish.

GABOON EBONY (Africa) is really a rusty brown-black. It is extremely expensive, and is available only in such small pieces as to make it very difficult to use.

MYRTLE BURL is a highly figured, very blonde wood of widely varying designs. It is susceptible to very interesting pattern matching.

POLLARD OAK is a rather small grained English oak of a brown color.

OLIVE WOOD from Italy, coming from a small tree, can be used only in closely matched patterns or as decorative offsets. There is an English ash sometimes called English Ash Olive Burl which partakes of the character of the Olive Burl of Italy.

PADOUK or VERMILION is an import from India. The color is brilliantly orange red on a pinky ground. Its brilliant color adapts it to highly decorative effects, although it would probably be excessive in a large piece of furniture.

PIQUA or BOSSE wood from Africa has a uniform

pink-brown color with a mottled satiny texture which finishes handsomely. The wood is successfully used for large veneered surfaces.

PURPLE HEART is also called AMARANTH or VIOLET WOOD. When the tree is cut the inner part, on being exposed to air, becomes a brilliant violet purple. On exposure to light it is apt to lose this purplish cast somewhat, but it is sufficiently exotic to warrant its occasional use for brilliant decorative purposes.

BRAZILIAN ROSEWOOD is a very hard and heavy wood, principally purply brown with almost black streaks. When the wood is freshly cut it exudes a smell like roses—hence the name. It was tremendously popular in the middle of the 19th century, and suffered a complete eclipse until recent years, when it has been revived for modern furniture and for reproductions.

The East India Rosewood is called by the French Palisander. On the continent it has been favored for modern furniture. It has a more definite combed grain stripe than the Brazilian Rosewood, and the color is rather more neutral. It takes a very high finish.

The Honduras Rosewood is a lighter, more uniformly grained specimen than the Brazilian Rosewood, but partakes of its characteristics of hardness and weight, with the accompanying possibility of surface cracking.

SAPELI is an African wood that closely resembles mahogany in color and texture, except that it is more evenly striped. This has made it popular with modern designers.

SATINWOOD from Ceylon or the East Indies is a highly figured, light yellow to golden brown wood which, as its name indicates, has a distinct satiny finish. It was widely used in French work and in the reproductions of that style.

The West Indian Satinwood has less of the stripe and blistered quality, but is a very agreeable wood where blonde effects are desired.

TAMO is the Japanese Ash. It has a wild figure in a blonde color.

ZEBRA WOOD or ZEBRANO, as its name implies, has a vigorous brown stripe on a light brown ground. It hails from Africa.

PRIMA VERA or WHITE MAHOGANY grows in Mexico and Guatemala. It has the grain of mahogany, but is a very pale brown about the color of birch. It is a handsome, easily worked wood, and could well be used more extensively.

TULIP WOOD is a Brazilian species, with red and purple stripes on a yellowish ground. It is no relation to the American Tulip Tree, which is really of the Magnolia family. It is used chiefly for inlays, on account of its small size.

TEAK is a very important wood in tropical sections where exposure to moisture and heat and insect attacks is a factor. It grows in India, Burma, Java and the Malay Peninsula. It is light tobacco brown in color. The blackish cast made familiar thru Oriental objects is only a stain.

FAUX SATINE or FALSE SATIN is a cypress veneer with a strongly decorative crotch effect.

REDWOOD BURLS or SEQUOIA are used considerably in modern work. They are small patterned and have a warm orange-brown color.

FIR is not at all adaptable for solid work for furniture, but is used for commercial plywood, interior trim, etc. The texture is very soft.

HAREWOOD has been one of the most popular woods for modern furnishing. It is the English Sycamore, dyed a silvery gray. It has a close curly figure and a dense grain, with a tendency to lose the dye on exposure to strong light.

ENGLISH SYCAMORE has been used considerably in modern work for its light pinkish tone.

CEDAR is rarely used for furniture.

PINE was used in most early American work, and in various European work, rarely for itself, but for its economy and ease of working. Recently there has been a vogue for "pickled pine," a whitish patina on knotty pine which originates from the habit of scraping off the paint from old English furniture. Pine was originally used for economy in these pieces, with the idea that the paint would cover the grain, but it was discovered, on removing some of the paint for re-finishing, that the surface remaining was quite interesting.

There are many woods, both domestic and imported, that are highly decorative but because of their scarcity or difficulty in working, are used to a limited extent and then only for the decorative effects produced by the veneers. This list by no means covers the possibilities. Every year some new wood springs into popularity, and might be widely advertised and with probably perfectly good reason. To cite a few, we have Carpathian Elm, Claro Walnut, Snakewood, etc.

The rarity of a wood is not necessarily an index to its cost in the finished product. Actually, with any veneer, the cost of the labor to apply it is far in excess of the wood itself. Outside of the burls and similar freaks which are extremely wasteful in handling and matching, the average woods in the above list do not vary widely in cost. Under present conditions, labor is the primary factor. A choice veneer of maple will usually be much more costly than an indifferent grade of mahogany or walnut, or even some of the less known names.

WOOD FINISHES

The finishing of wood is finally the application to the raw wood of a protective film. This film holds down the fibers of the wood and seals the pores which would otherwise tend to absorb moisture. The basis of finish is therefore a gum, of one variety or another, held in suspension in a volatile liquid. Linseed oil, tung oil, etc., are typical gums; various compounds of gums, volatiles and colors produce varnish, lacquer, shellac, paint, enamel, etc. The first essential of the film is toughness and elasticity; other properties will vary with differing requirements. Thus while the technically better finish has a full body, the preference is for minimum finish which leaves the "woody" quality. Wood finishes are struggling for a happy medium between the old "varnished" look with its full durable body, and unvarnished dull look that displays the wood texture better but lacks permanence and thus fails to protect the wood.

All wood finishes tend to darken the natural color of raw wood. Many processes exist for the modification of the original color of wood as well as to offset the effect of finish on the color of wood. Bleaching by chemicals is extensively practised; many fashionable shades of walnut, oak, mahogany, etc., are produced by this process. Pigmenting or filling the pores of wood with color produces a range of shades and textures; washes or "glazes" of semi-opaque color produce similar effects but diminish textural quality.

Sandblasting and combing are used on strongly grained woods to produce high textures, which in turn are often emphasized with pigment.

WILLOW, WICKER AND FIBRE

These materials are comparatively without strength in themselves and depend upon a more rigid framework of wood or metal. Furniture made of them is light and cool looking, and therefore used for tropical and summer purposes. Its design cannot but grow out of its limitations; it is variously bent or woven into the desired shapes. Sharp corners are eliminated.

No matter what style influence this type of furniture is based upon, it looks primarily like its material; it is therefore preferable to keep the forms as simple and direct as possible. Chinese and East Indian work exhibit good functional forms, pleasantly designed.

Rush or flag for seating is a long grass, twisted and woven. It occurs in the provincial chairs of every country. As the material dries it decomposes, and it should therefore be well coated with shellac or paint.

Cane is a very satisfactory material for seats and layer surfaces where an effect of lightness is wanted. It is yielding and comfortable, inexpensive and offers interesting possibilities of texture.

METALS IN FURNITURE

While metal has always been in the furniture designer's kit, it remained for the modern movement to revalue it and to exploit it extensively. We find metal furniture in the ancient work, and it was very considerably used throughout the Renaissance in Italy and Spain. Because of the great weight, however, it was principally used as accessory to wood. In Spanish and Italian work it was employed for stretchers and similar structural members as well as trimming.

Wrought iron was the outstanding metal of that time, although there was some bronze. Under the Louis's in France, bronze and brass attained greater importance and were widely used but only as decorative offsets and usually with a clear gilt finish called ormolu.

There are in every period and style some examples of various metal work but these are inclined to be minor. In America of the early 19th century iron casting was a vital art. It not only flowered into all manner of benches and chairs and tables, principally for outdoor use, but a very considerable fauna, without which the recollection of no childhood is complete. Of course, these were pretty ponderous affairs, and not really designed to be moved. They should be classed as cemetery art rather than furniture.

With the advent of liberated thinking along furniture lines came the use of tubular steel sections. The most outstanding success from every point of view is the steel chair, which faintly resembles the figure 5 with the top bar missing. This chair is light and springy, not easily damaged, and will ultimately be produced very inexpensively. It has become common practice to plate the metal chromium, but this need as yet not necessarily be so, except that no more satisfactory finish has as yet appeared.

This chair is at once an outstanding success of modern design, and also its most vulnerable point for attack, from which we can conclude that it represents a new approach to design through utilizing a material for what it is in itself, rather than for what it can be made to look like.

The antithesis of this idea occurs in the attempt to use aluminum for the traditional form of chairs. While the various arguments offered for its sale are undoubtedly true, the answer seems to be that that style is perfectly good when executed in wood, and that the aluminum contributes nothing in proportion to its greater cost.

In a similar manner tubular steel has been used for an infinite variety of supports, and there is nothing to be said against this practice except that it offends the eye unaccustomed to this form, with the consequent risk of incurring ridicule as "plumbing" furniture. It might be worth mentioning at this point that criticism can very easily discover unfavorable analogies. People with the courage of their likes and dislikes should have the courage to resist that kind of ridicule, which is facile and corrosive.

All the tubular type of furniture is based on the essential strength of steel. It would be definitely impractical to use copper tubing for structural forms, although brass tubing under some conditions is strong enough. Flat sections, bars and other solid sections will bend or spring more easily than tubular sections of equivalent sizes.

Metals, of course, are either hot or cold to the touch, so that it is undesirable to have contact points of plain metal. On the other hand, color and texture of metal can always be used as an interesting contrast with other materials.

Metals used as surface materials are susceptible to a wide range of color treatments. Contrast, even in the slight difference of texture produced by brushing or scratching metals in different ways, gives it an interesting pattern. Aluminum, bronze, brass, copper, pewter, stainless steel, nickel, cast iron, monel metal, etc. are in varying degrees all useful for decorative or structural purposes, and there seems to be little doubt that the field of metal furniture has wide possibilities.

Of course, in designing combinations of furniture involving metal with other materials, as wood and glass, there is at present a grave danger of disregarding the basic principles of joinery. No metal and wood joint can ever be as strong as a wood-to-wood joint, as it will depend on screws, which have a tendency to loosen with vibration. The old notion that metal is strong leads to mistaken confidence in metal furniture. True, the metal itself is strong, but the strength of a piece of furniture is not so much in the materials as *in the joints*. The problem is infinitely aggravated when we join glass with metal. While much furniture is being offered in this medium at present, it is doubtful if this style will persist without the invention of some better method of obtaining cohesion between the parts.

GLASS IN FURNITURE

The current vogue for new materials in furniture has forced the hand of the designer. The market is full of creations involving the greater or lesser use of glass. Most of them should be approached gingerly by buyers hoping for durability. Glass is difficult to join tightly with metal or wood. It is safest when used loosely, lying in a bed made of the other material.

It should be remembered that glass is one of the hardest possible surfaces. Dining tables with glass tops produce unpleasant sounds and might be blamed for considerable breakage of china and table glass. Of course it cannot be denied that there is no surface as resistant to liquid and some other forms of damage, so that before deprecating its use for tops too thoroughly, its value in small or occasional tables, drink tables, dressing tables, etc., is not only recognized but advocated. Its brilliance and transparency are so desirable under some conditions that one may overlook its faults.

Glass in colors, both as mirrors and transparent tops, is also tellingly decorative. There is a wide field for glass with etching, engraving, mitre cutting, sand blasting, etc. But these functions are rather more specialized than this book can discuss.

Vitrolite and Carrara glass are trade names for opaque glass which generally comes in thick slabs and can be used with very good effect.

Mirrors have been the decorators' ace since the 17th century. Apart from their value for actual reflection, they multiply images of light and dark, producing an effect of brilliance and unlimited space. For catching and trapping light in dark spaces, for increasing vistas, to create the illusion of size or depth, or for any manipulation of light and perspective, mirrors are in a class by themselves.

The possibilities of glass in decoration are growing greater daily. The new house forms are often predicated largely on great glass areas. These may be clear glass, glass bricks, or the various semi-transparent or translucent glasses. There is a double glass with an air space for transparent insulation; there are tempered or laminated glasses for doors and structural uses. For the most part these developments are in the hands of the architects, and to their credit be it said that they are meeting the expanding usefulness of glass with judgment, tact and restraint.

PLASTICS

Possibly the widest scope for experiment with new possibilities for furniture is in the field of plastics. This comprises all the multitudes of materials streaming from the laboratory—casein products, celluloid and nitrocellulose developments, phenol resins, etc. These are more familiarly known by trade names, among which are Bakelite, Micarta, Formica, Lucite, Plexiglass, etc.

The Bakelite, Micarta and Formica types are generally thin veneer, which is applied to wood panels and used as tops, etc. They have the virtue of being highly resistant to heat and fire, destructive liquids, scratching, etc. They are chiefly opaque, and available in a wide range of colors and simulated textures like fabrics, woods and marble. These materials are also offered in bars, tubes, etc., so that many small articles may be fabricated.

A special development in this field is the treatment of actual wood with transparent plastic so that the texture is retained. Used for highly resistant top surfaces it is both decorative and durable.

Lucite and Plexiglass are even more astounding. These are crystal clear plastics of great intrinsic beauty. They have most of the properties of glass plus some extraordinary ones, like peculiar transmission of light. They have great structural strength, are not difficult to join, can be carved or formed into objects of beauty, with or without surface decoration or modelling. The surface is too soft to be used for table tops, etc., and the cost is still quite high.

Of course the idea of plastics suggests that they be molded, not fabricated, and their real field lies in the production of articles made in large quantities. Thus a proper exploitation of plastics in furniture is still limited to extremely small articles like radio cases and accessory parts. Much has been written and spoken of plastics in furniture but there are still too few examples of furniture that is better for being made of plastic than of other materials. The frenzy of plastics in chairs, tables, etc., shows us no new technique or usefulness; the mere novelty rarely seems to justify the added expense and ingenuity of construction. Aesthetically its use appears questionable when strained into mere echoes—or spectres—of wood designs and construction.

Lest this appear to be merely querulous, let it be said that it is quite impossible for material of such beauty to be long misunderstood. Quite certainly designers will appear who will utilize the special qualities and techniques of these materials, to enlarge and grace our decorative repertoire.

Rubber, linoleum and cork are likewise used for table tops and desk tops and bases, with considerable success, having some properties of resistance which make them valuable for special uses. Nursery tables with rubber tops, linoleum or rubber tops for office desks, cork tops for end tables, etc., are other examples of specialized uses.

CHAPTER XVI

FABRICS

All fabrics are constructed by the interlacing of vertical threads (warp) with horizontal threads (weft).

If this interlacing is simply under and over we have a plain weave—vertical lines regularly crossed at every intersection by horizontal lines.

If the horizontal thread covers two vertical threads, then goes under two vertical threads, we have a twill weave—an effect of diagonal lines as in serges.

When the horizontal thread covers three vertical threads, goes under one, then over three more or vice versa, we have a satin weave in which either the bulk of warp threads or the bulk of weft threads shows on the surface.

It is obvious that there are innumerable combinations and variations possible as to pattern and texture by using complex weaves, various thicknesses of various materials, and of course by using different colors of materials.

However, if you examine any piece of cloth and the reverse of it, you will be able to determine which basic weave or combination of weaves was used in its manufacture.

The materials referred to in this chapter are the fibres used in upholstery fabrics. Those commonly encountered are cotton, silk, wool, rayon, linen, mohair, ramie, and jute. Cellophane has been used for interesting effects against light and also somewhat in upholstering. Asbestos might conceivably find an adaptation, as might anything that can be woven. But the eight above-mentioned fibres in various combinations and weaves are the materials that give us the important fabrics and textiles we use in decoration. The variety of effects obtained by manipulation of the weaves is multiplied by the variety of materials and their possibilities in combination. Sheen, roughness, strength, lightness, and all the gradations arise chiefly from the handling of these two factors, weave and material, which constitute the construction features of the fabric.

And a still further multiplication of possibilities is developed in the finishing of the fabrics. Finishing includes dyeing, printing, bleaching, shrinking and all sorts of special processes like batik, moire, etc.

We have emphasized the infinite variety in fabrics, so that the choice is almost without limit. The selection available to any one person is only a small part of the realm of textiles. Almost any effect may be achieved. And the aforementioned cellophane fabric is typical of imaginative fabric usage.

The general principles elsewhere discussed in this book will apply with particular force to the use of textiles in decoration. Consider the usage. Don't use flimsy cloth for articles that must stand wear. Consider the colors. Remember that the color appearance will be different for different weaves, materials and finishes. Consider the texture and the texture scheme and effect. Smooth textures tend to be formal, rough tend to be informal. And there should be a harmony in textures in each room—not only of textiles but of all other surfaces.

The list of fabrics given below is by no means complete, but it contains most of the usual varieties used in decoration.

UNFIGURED FABRICS .

There is an infinite variety of beautiful unfigured fabrics created by manipulation of the factors of fibre and weave. These unfigured types include reps, cords, loose basket weaves, cloister cloth, shikii, taffetas, changeable silks, imberline, striaé and jaspé.

Moire is an unfigured type but its effect is achieved in the finishing rather than in weaving. These cloths will all vary in strength, texture, purpose and no general recommendation may be made about its texture.

Damask. A fabric with raised figured designs, the lines of which run in a different direction from the background lines. Usually it is woven in one color and mostly silk but occasionally it occurs in cotton, wool, linen, etc., and sometimes in contrasting colors. It is largely used for drapery and upholstery and generally though not always it is reversible. Cotton and linen damasks are most used for napery.

Brocatelles are a variation of damask but the figures are raised more and have more of the velvet quality. Figures are generally large and bold and this fabric is therefore more suitable for large public rooms rather than homes.

Brocades are different from damask and brocatelles

in that they are infinitely varicolored. They resemble hand embroidery.

Velvet, Velours, Plush, Frieze. These are pile fabrics that are popularly deemed to stand for luxury. Though usually silk they may be made of the other fibres. Velvet is compact, velour has the rows of pile wide apart and more visible. Plush is deep pile velvet. Frieze (bouclé) is an uncut velvet, generally woven of linen, wool or mohair rather than silk. It is very durable.

Chintz and Cretonne. These are printed cloths. Chintz is lighter and has small patterns. Cretonne is heavier with larger patterns. Chintz is sometimes glazed to produce a glassy surface which provides high lights and is substantially dustproof.

Tapestry is important because of the advantages of design, beauty and extreme durability. There are three schools of tapestry design—the Gothic, Brussels and the Gobelin. Many are still hand woven.

Armure is a ribbed silk or cotton fabric with a small design on the surface.

Grosgrain is a heavy ribbed taffeta.

Mohair is a wool-like fibre used for many upholstery and drapery effects. It is derived from the fleece of angora goats.

Panne is a pile fabric which has been flattened so that the pile lies close to the back. This gives the shiny appearance.

Poplin is a fine woven fabric of silk or lustrous cotton with light cross ribs.

Rep is a ribbed fabric made of silk, mercerized cotton or wool with fine warp threads to cover the entire surface.

Satin is a weave in which the bulk of the warp or weft is predominantly on the face of the fabric. It is often referred to as a material though technically is is a weave.

Taffeta is a plain smooth silk fabric with the same count warp and weft.

LEATHER

Leather has come into decided favor in recent years. It can be dyed or lacquered to any desired shade, and the finer leathers have a very agreeable, soft texture. The steer hide, or cowhide, source of most leather used for upholstering, is split into a number of thicknesses from the original hide. The top hide, or the layer immediately under the thin top layer, is the best for furniture, being lightest in weight, toughest in texture, and softest feeling. The cuts beneath this are artificially surfaced and textured, and therefore the surface is more uniform and lacks the individual variations and oddities that contribute to the interest of the top grain.

Pigskin, goatskin, moroccos, kid, suede, etc., are occasionally used, but the large steer hide is most generally employed in upholstery and decorative work. A special process produces a rawhide of exceptional textural interest.

The textures of one leather are frequently reproduced in others. The characteristic dots of pigskin are impressed into steerhide; likewise the morocco grain, or shark grain, or any other texture can be developed.

Imitation leathers vary from cheap oil cloths to the very high grade materials which cost almost as much as leather.

Leathers have been used as wall coverings since primitive times. The practice has been revived with much interest, and modern rooms with leather walls have been successful. The special finishes applied to leather now encourage its use for the tops and fronts of tables, chests, etc. with more security than in similar usage in past times. Leathers so used may be tacked down and studded, or glued taut. The latter method often suggests tooled designs embossed into the surface and gilded or otherwise embellished.

CHAPTER XVII

WALL COVERINGS

Stone walls are the most archaic. Formal rooms such as pompous foyers and galleries still use them. Sandstone, Caen Stone, travertine, marble, have all been incorporated into the grand type of interior.

Very early it was found more comfortable to have a fabric on the cold stone, and this evolved into the pictorial tapestry. The use of fabrics was extended to the hanging of brocades and silks. These were finally pasted on and became the inspiration for some wall papers. Printed and painted fabrics were hung, pasted or framed in panels in the 18th century.

Wall papers came with the extension of French influence to China, and were widely favored in the 18th century. The earliest were Chinese themes, but the French broke away and initiated their own patterns. They have been continually in use since then. Today, we have flat colors, stripes, abstract patterns, more or less simple ornamental motifs, reproductions of fabrics and woods and large scenic reproductions which cover whole walls with a single theme.

Domino papers out of 16th century Italy are small marbleized sheets arranged in patterns.

Paint and plaster finishes are chiefly a matter of color and texture. Paints may be flat or glossy or stippled to yield a vibrant texture; glazed over with another tone, or mottled for irregular effects. Plaster may be smooth or treated to numerous processes to produce an assortment of textures. Sand Float, trowelling, and Craftex effects are adaptable to each style.

Wood panelling came in corollary to fabrics, as a buffer to the cold stone. Wood walls have a pleasing quality, and occur in more or less ornate forms in all styles. Oak, walnut, pine, mahogany, and chestnut occur in traditional work; modern wood panelling uses even very rare veneers. An excellently simulated wood surface is Flexwood, actual veneer applied to fabric and cemented to the wall. They permit the covering of large surfaces without breaks and are valuable on curved work.

Molding panels grew from the wood panelling habit. Bolection moldings applied to plaster sometimes create a spirit of architectural composition.

Moldings in one form or another have always been an essential architectural feature of a room, and almost any period room can be made to hint of architectural importance with a discreet use of decorative moldings. Of course the modern work eschews molding entirely as tending to disturb planes and insinuate unrelated pattern in the background. But the use of some of the wallboards mentioned below automatically indicates the use of moldings to conceal or accent the joints of these panels. For this purpose in modern work, metal and contrasting wood moldings have been widely employed, and special metal moldings of aluminum and copper have been developed for just this purpose.

We can only mention the whole field of mural painting and fresco work, and we should call attention to a new one that is being very intelligently used for decoration and purposes of illusion—the enlarged photograph, or photomural, varying from abstract patterns to photographic replicas of views, all of which create illusions of depth or size where none exist.

Tiles, plain or decorative, have a definite style sense. The Moors brought them to Spain, whence they spread all over Europe.

Wallboards of various types have been purely structural, but recently several have been marketed which have textures interesting enough in themselves. Presdwood and Celotex either in the natural state or some of the decorative finishes offered may be used with interesting results.

Linoleum applied like wall paper is now advocated as a wall covering where hard usage is expected. Some simulate wood or stone, and are satisfactory for foyers, bathrooms, game rooms, nurseries, etc. They are easily applied, easily cleaned and withstand more than the ordinary blows and scratches.

Mirrors for walls are not new. Heroic things are being done with mirrors, both clear and colored types. Too much cannot be said for a thoughtful and studied placing of mirrors for emphasizing perspective and vistas and introducing light into dark spots. Colored mirrors accomplish special ends. Gunmetal mirrors produce a shadowy depth. Pink mirrors create a warm brilliance. Blue mirrors will yield a sense of cool distance. Mirrors are an important tool to the decorator for the creation of architectural illusion, as color, and for light.

CEILINGS

We have overdecorated walls and floors and neglected ceilings. Not that ornamentation is recommended for general use, but we cannot just let the ceiling go as a bare spot.

In following traditional ways, we find an appropriate ceiling treatment for every style, integrating the ornamental aspect of all the planes. In many good traditional rooms, the most common give-away comes when the eye passes the cornice line and we see a pure out-and-out 20th century composition of fireproofed beams and girders grand and unashamed. Slight additional expense will permit the furring down of the ceiling, or an ingenious division of spaces and levels that harmonizes with the style chosen. In many styles, beams are a distinct feature and may be played up.

Modern solutions avowedly emanate from the structure, so the beams and projections will be no problem. They can be further utilized for the development of diffused general lighting. Again, remembering that much of the color characteristics of a room derive from the light reflected from the ceiling, we can do things about tinting or coloring this plane that will be of profound assistance in throwing a single harmonizing cast over all the objects and colors in a room.

Low small rooms, as entries, foyers and hallways may have the ceiling's height reduced in order to create by contrast a sense of higher ceilings in adjoining important rooms. This may be accomplished by furring down or by the use of a deep lowering color, such as gray or blue.

CHAPTER XVIII

FLOOR COVERINGS

The range of floor coverings includes such structural elements as wood, tile, stone and marble, cement and composition to those that are extremely decorative, such as fine Oriental rugs. Rubber, rubber tile, linoleum and composition floors may be used over any existing floor.

Factors in choice of floorings are the use required, expense, color, warmth, cleanliness, durability, sound properties, and the degree of luxury. For semi-outside rooms such as vestibules and foyers, a decorative, hard wearing material is recommended. Tiles and marble or thin linoleum and rubber counterparts are entirely satisfactory. Kitchen, bathroom, nurseries, play rooms etc., where frequent washing is necessary will also utilize such materials. As they contribute an air of coolness, all such hard non-porous coverings should be used in conservatories and sun rooms.

The reverse condition recommends carpets for living room, bedrooms and all the more intimate rooms in the colder climates. In cities especially, the noise-absorbing quality of carpeting recommends it. Carpeting covering the entire floor has the effect of enlarging a room.

The qualities of carpeting in order of cost are: Chenille, Wilton, Axminster, Velvets, Brussels, Tapestries, and Ingrain. Any kind may be plain colored, self patterned or have vari-colored designs. They may be Oriental, European or domestic. They may be high or low pile and of a variety of textures. The choice of carpets is therefore no simple matter for rules.

Broadloom merely refers to the width in which the carpet is woven without seams. Strip carpet is narrow, either 27 or 36 inches, and may be sewed together to form large surfaces. As the cost of sewing almost equals the extra cost of the wide looming, the broadloom is much more popular.

Every form of pattern is woven into rugs and carpeting today, for any style of decoration. There are reproductions of hooked rugs, Persians, Chinese, Aubusson and Savonnerie. The house decorator has no excuse for using an inappropriate floor covering.

Patented back carpeting is joined together by a type of adhesive tape which adheres to the special base of the carpet. This replaces sewing and permits the actual inlaying of designs just as it would be done in wood or linoleum.

Undercarpets are most desirable. They are made of various combinations of hair and jute. They increase the resilience and softness of carpeting and add to its durability.

Oriental carpets are always handmade in the definite traditional designs, weaves, and colors of the locale from which the types take their names. Few indeed are the reliable connoisseurs in this field, and the wise buyer yields to the advice of a trusted dealer.

Fine rugs from the East were one of the first articles of import into Europe after the Crusades, and have taken a prominent position in the decorative scheme of every period. According to their qualities, they are rich and elegant to a superlative degree. A fine rug may well be inspiration for an entire room. A small one may center a grouping, and may be used over a base of solid carpeting. There is rarely any excuse for laying a loose rug other than parallel to the walls.

A modern room even of radical design may utilize a good Oriental rug. In most designs the pattern is so abstract and emanates so clearly from the weaving technique that it will fit admirably.

There are many other hand woven types of rugs that will similarly stand up well in a modern design. The Navajo with its clear color and sharp abstractions, Druggets with a varied texture and geometric pattern, and hooked rugs of geometric design, are all satisfactory where used with taste.

Almost too numerous to mention are the varieties of woven floorings now available. Linen, cotton, grass, wool, cellophane, jute and hemp, paper and what not are woven into strong, more or less decorative floorings. Designs reflecting every taste are printed, painted, woven or stamped into them.

Linoleum will vary from very cheap oil cloth with printed pattern to heavy linoleums which have either all-over color or inserted patterns. These are usually cemented to the floor; sometimes, in the plain colors, designed with inlays, designs, stripes or similar decorative motifs. Linoleum patterns often simulate tile, which make them interesting for recreation rooms, tap rooms, indoor garden rooms, conservatories and foyers.

Rubber comes in sheet form and is treated like linoleum, or as rubber tiling which is laid down in small blocks and produces about the same decorative effect as stone or tile floors.

Cork is laid in small blocks like tiles. It has the virtue of being highly heat absorbing, which makes it comfortable for all rooms. It is silent, and takes an agreeable brownish color when waxed.

Tile, marble and hard and synthetic materials like Zenitherm are occasionally used for special purposes, as are plastic substances that are trowelled on, like cement and wood floors, either plain, inlaid or parquetry. Woods used in this fashion are maple, oak, pine, walnut, and hard woods. Parquet floors have herringbone, diamond shapes or squares of small pieces laid in a sort of mosaic or plaid pattern.

Straight floors are made of long, narrow boards, sometimes with a border or other design woven in around the side.

Finishes vary from a very simple coating of wax to a highly varnished surface.

Painted wood floors are found in many styles. The early American and Federal periods especially produced some interesting deviations from straight painting, such as spatter-dash and pebbling.

CHAPTER XIX

DECORATIVE OBJECTS

Decorative objects and the architecture of the room are not strictly related. It might be said that the use of decorative objects as such would tend to confuse the design of the actual room, architecturally speaking. The more current feeling, however, is that these incidental features create a sense of personal warmth, either through the distraction afforded the eye, or the sense of familiarity engendered by the repetition of unimportant themes.

There is a vast category that might be included within the field of decorative objects; in fact, everything that partakes of a non-structural or non-utilitarian nature may be bracketed under this heading. Paintings and sculpture, ornaments, vases, bowls, ash trays, clocks, all have a varying degree of usefulness and individually ornamental character.

As a general principle, ornaments placed without impairing the feeling of space or usefulness of the room may be considered acceptable, if not positively good. They need not necessarily extend or confine themselves to the particular period characteristics of the room, because they are not chosen with relation to it, any more than the bindings of books in a modern room must all be modern.

These adornments of the room should be regarded

as the most personal expression of the owner, in the same way that the adornments worn on the person are intimate and cherished beyond the actual clothing. To use ornaments for their own sake is an empty practice. To use in their ornamental capacity objects which have a degree of personal association with the individual who dominates the room, elevates the whole practice beyond the scope of the interior decorator to criticize. It is not for the decorator to say that photographs may or may not be part of a room. Indeed, a fragment of the rock of Gibraltar or a souvenir of Niagara Falls might have decorative value to an individual as a connotation or a recollection, and should not be barred. To rule out the cherished moss of a rolling stone creates a stilted atmosphere, at least to the rolling stone. It deprives him of his freest expression, and ultimately makes him hate his room.

Of course, most accumulations will represent more virtue than these examples. It is really more likely that the average person will, more or less mistakenly, cherish what is believed to have artistic value. Even this point is immune to criticism, but if there is something of beauty in the intrinsic character of the thing that bears exploitation, it would be a mistake not to feature it and even expand on the idea offered. The wise decorator, rather than be baffled by difficult souveniers, will find some way of absorbing them, so that they do not protrude in the composition. The high point of this approach will be from the ownership of a work of art—a painting or a piece of sculpture, a fine Oriental rug, or an ancient Chinese horse. In a way, the better the art, the more universal it will be, and the wider the variety of backgrounds that will provide a suitable harmony. A Goya, or a Ming porcelain may have an honored place in a wholly abstruse modern room or in the most vibrant Quatrocento reproduction. Indeed, should you be the fortunate possessor of something so good, as your own decorator you could do no better than to consider this bit of virtu the inspiration of your entire room.

Rooms having more than one very important object of this nature would do well to arrange for each one some distinctive background that will permit its supremacy, even if only in its corner; but if the collection attains such numbers that this becomes impossible, you must frankly make your room a gallery, with the other functions subservient.

PICTURES

Pictures will be the most general application of this idea. A fine picture should be valued to the extent of letting it influence the color scheme, whether in a complementary or derivative way. It will follow that the framing of the picture will have to be considered similarly. The tendency in modern paintings is to frame simply, often with wash colors on the frames, derived from the low tones of the picture. Prints will be treated similarly, important colored ones being framed without glass.

The height of the picture is a particularly sensitive point. It should have a set relation within the rectangle on which it hangs so that it cuts out an agreeable shape. It should not hang too high to be looked at easily, nor too low. Generally a bit above the eye line for the center of the picture is desirable.

If a number of pictures have related themes which would permit groupings, such as etchings or a series of prints, they should be similarly framed and hung closely in such a way as to form a composition together, rather than singly.

There will be spaces in a room that will be greatly enhanced as compositions by the use of a picture, and sometimes even a foil for the picture, in the form of a bowl or another decorative spot that will compose with the picture.

Where there is a pronounced architectural or traditional aspect to the room, the frames may well be considered part of the architecture. Often a large picture can be given a firm architectural base in the form of a long low bookcase or other furniture which keeps it from being too "skyed." It is unwise to buy pictures to go with the color scheme of the room. If the picture is fine, it may serve as the basis for the color scheme. No rules about adherence to period requirements govern such conditions.

The historical note may be enlivened by clever selection of pictures. Currier & Ives or Hogarth, French engravings and reprints of Italian primitives, may be quite at home in a background with which they are associated.

In a day not long past it was considered essential to have pictures on walls. This is a better day for decorators, for people buy pictures because they like them and not because they are afraid of blank walls. The individual's preference is the governing factor, not a fear that an expanse of unadorned space violates a rule. Much happier the Japanese custom of hanging no pictures except for stated occasions. The best guest gets the best pictures, which are unrolled from their cases and hung only during his presence. It is probably true that we no longer see a picture after the whole composition has thoroughly imbedded itself in our minds. If, for the picture's sake, we want to keep it alive, it might be better to move it occasionally to varying lights, or to put it away at intervals, and replace it with another.

SCULPTURE

Very largely, the same general ideas will apply to pieces of sculpture. Sculpture is conceived and executed in the round, and should be visible from several angles. Reliefs, of course, may be treated as pictures.

One way of getting this variety of viewpoint for sculpture is to place it in a sort of a reflecting surface. The material of the sculpture should be the determining factor, not its base. It is generally undesirable to repeat in the plinth the colors of the sculptured material, as this causes the whole feeling of the thing to flow down instead of concentrating its interest in the work.

It is entirely possible, and most interesting, to work out some object of furniture as a base, rather than the mortuary pedestal on which the Carrara laughing boys and dying nymphs breathed and rested a generation ago.

Sculptures, being compositions entirely in light and shade, must have a composed surface behind them. If a mirror is used, it must not carry too many other re-flections or the object is defeated.

Wall paintings, mural decoration, or photographic murals present a different problem. After you buy a picture you find a place for it. But a mural is approached just as self-consciously as the carpet on the floor. It should be considered as a wall treatment, for the essential character of a mural is flatness. Thus it must be planned as part of the original composition of the room.

The display of ornaments wholly without decorative intrinsic, or reminiscent value is discouraged most heartily. The capricious animals and eccentricities that appear every day are like good jokes, enjoyable when heard once. Objects of a more sincere artistic impulse—vases and bowls and similar accessories—have always been important, and can be mixed with considerable freedom. A collection of Chinese porcelains will grace any room, but it is important to incorporate them in some way into a whole rather than have them strewn about where they perpetually give the sense of being something to knock over or catch dust.

Taste is the one quality that enters into the mixing of period ornaments. Chinese art has a universal quality, because it is not identified in our minds with any specific period. The less glaringly dated an ornament, the wider its scope of application. To us, Chinese objects fall so much into one category that we can use them without offense in almost any kind of room, yet a highly ornamented Sevres vase will not only fail to blend readily into any French room. but to a refined discrimination it may not even blend in every French room of its own period.

We can only say that taste and the basic, always vital sense of fitness is the only criterion. Your room may express *you* more clearly through the ornaments and the unconscious gesture than in all the studied artfulness of composition and color harmony.

The desirability of brilliance makes it more than desirable to consider the use of glass and pottery bowls as vases and ornaments. The need for accents will be felt individually, and this can be trusted to the intuition of the decorator more readily than anything else.

There is in each material available for this purpose an inherent quality. Glass in the plainest surfaces is still brilliant. It is therefore a mistake, usually, to have it ornate. We find in many rooms a great deal of glass being shown on shelves across the windows—a brilliant and witty conceit which brings in touches of highlight and color. Fine glazes in themselves have a richness and interest entirely adequate for whatever decorative purpose they may be required; it is like gilding the lily to make the shape complex.

Silver, gold, bronze, pewter, copper, brass, chromium, lead—every metal has in itself such vital personality that it should be freely expressed when used in these decorative spots. The rightness of any metal, glaze or other material, to the room in which it is going to be used, is a matter of color scheme, composition and the whole spirit of the room. It is not recommended that objects be merely lined up on a shelf—pairs and squadrons of bowls and vases on a metal shelf or window sill. Unless the vase has tremendous interest in itself, it were far better kept in the pantry except when filled with flowers.

It would probably be a little too blank and bare to have a room without any ornaments whatsoever, but an increased number or variety may diminish rather than enhance the effectiveness of the room. Ash trays and clocks, fire tongs and andirons, bookends and desk sets, sofa pillows and similar utilitarian objects should be content to be entirely direct. The Scotty on the ash tray contributes very little, especially if the ash tray part is too flat. And incidentally, most ash trays are too small.

Clocks have always been a decorative feature, and can be found in suitable styles for every period. The monumental clock has a place in monumental interiors only. Generally speaking, it is the camel in the tent, taking up room out of proportion to its services. Clocks may be considered as articles of furniture when they are treated in cases like furniture. As to clocks, andirons, all useful things, the object of giving them decorative treatment is to make them merge into the background. When they become so emphatic that they emerge from the background, they are out of place.

This is the essence of the critique of ornaments. The effort to disguise telephones, switch plates and faucets, by means of ornamentation, is generally unsuccessful.

MUSICAL INSTRUMENTS

Musical instruments represent crystallized forms with which it would be dangerous to experiment. The shapes are accepted, and are the outgrowth of the musicians' demands, not the decorator's. They should accordingly be honored as such. The piano and the harp are the principal objects of concern in this field, and the best thing the decorator can do in a room that shelters one of these instruments is either to bow to the inevitable and make it a feature as it stands, if the room is not large enough to bestow it upon a corner, or to make it a feature frankly expressive of one of the activities of the room. In neither case does it facilitate the procedure to try to make it look like something else, or to worry too much about endowing it with the decorative character of the rest of the room. Pianos are now available in a variety of woods which ease the problem slightly by avoiding too abrupt a break in the color scheme. The upright piano is out of favor technically and artistically, since it is too large to lose itself and apparently not a good enough piano.

The practice of draping a piano or using it as a platform for a vase or a lamp is bad. It interferes with the performance of the instrument, it detracts from what rather elegant solidity the instrument has in itself, and it always has to be handled when the lid is lifted.

There is one general rule about objects of usefulness that are questionably decorative, such as pianos and telephones;—they are not improved by being further ornamented or disguised, and usually are made worse. If a piano is homely, it has an honest useful homeliness. The problem of the harp is rare; when it appears, most frequently in the homes of those who play it, the dominance of the instrument dictates that the composition flow from it.

The sources of mechanical music must be considered in an entirely different light. The radio and the phonograph have rarely been successfully treated as articles of furniture. They have been poured into every conceivable kind of case and table, the success of which depends upon the ability of a good piece of furniture to hide a radio.

There is nothing really wrong with this approach, except that a much better one might be made by hiding the mechanical features amid less selfconsciousness. Almost invariably a radio can be so submerged in bookcases or recesses of walls that they need represent no problem. If, however, the expense of such special adaptation is prohibitive, the simpler the box the better.

In modern rooms acceptance of the use of radio should be as fundamental as the acceptance of the new lighting. There is something mysteriously beautiful about the glow of radio tubes and the work they perform, and it is not unlikely that the future will yield some technique of making this part of the decorative expression. It should be borne in mind that the radio and speaker must be detachable without technical difficulty. Likewise, the phonograph may be connected to the radio for better performance as well as the simplification of both instruments. If the phonograph is used there should be as accessory to it some provision for a library of records. Records are better kept in a sort of bookcase which is definitely built-in.

SCREENS

In one form or another there have always been screens, and now they find expression in new forms. The essentials of the screen, beyond its being opaque, are that it be reasonably portable yet solid when placed.

Highly decorative screens are admissible in rooms where their function is originally decorative; where they are designed to divert the eye it would seem to be a mistake to call attention to them too violently. The screen that conceals the pantry door in the dining room should be unobtrusive, very solid, and partake of the general decorative feeling of the walls. Where screens are used to relieve monotony, to provide a balance or new planes, they may reach any height of fantasy. In extremely modern rooms, the screen has further taken the use of actual partitions. Semi-fixed screens may partially divide a room and create an illusion of depth.

The flexible screen that may be rolled and twisted at will is a particularly adaptable form, with very considerable decorative value. Screens from the Far East, like other Oriental art, have an unspecialized connotation that makes them acceptable to a wide field of period decoration.

LIVING PLANTS

Living plants have a way of reappearing on the decorative horizon. The natural form seems to satisfy some fundamental craving for relief from the excess of manufactured forms that fill most of our rooms.

While it might be safe to found a composition on the *Ficus Pandorata* or such major greenery, every year or two brings a new vogue in important potted plants. These are generally acceptable to the extent that they do humanize and lend grace and color. An increasing tendency is toward providing window gardens to brighten the life of the city dweller, an echo of our grandmothers' rows of geraniums in the bay window. Now the apartment gardener begins with a tiny collection in front of a sunny window and sometimes achieves the heights of a glassed-in cube in which temperature and humidity are controlled.

The Japanese have attained such a degree of sensitivity in the use of flowers and growing things, that for any interior we can safely study and borrow from their technique of composition. The simplest design prefers one perfect specimen to a large group.

Cut flowers likewise may be handled restrainedly, to the greater glorification of any decorative scheme. Even more than in growing plants, cut flowers offer us a palette of emphasis and contrast and brilliance that is changeable from day to day, to moods and occasions.

There are few occasional rooms that might have such a positive aggressive color scheme that certain flowers would not be usable, but for the average room every flower has a value. There are certain rooms in themselves architecturally satisfactory that become warm and inviting and superlative with the presence of some flowers or greenery. Even simple laurel leaves and huckleberry leaves contribute the broken lines that enrich and make valuable the flatness of plaster and wood. If it is presupposed that flowers will help a room there should be provision for flowers—vases and space to stand them on.

CHAPTER XX

COLOR

Color, like Truth and Beauty, is hard to define. Two people can rarely see color exactly alike, and the habit of using color names and terminology loosely makes it worse. An accepted scale or common key has made musical intervals and terms universally understood, but there is no such coordinated agreement about color. We have no basis of measurement for color, but there are a few names that are accepted.

We must first distinguish between the color of light and the color of pigment or material. Our concern is chiefly with the latter. Nothing better emphasizes the difference between the two than this:

The mixture of the pigment colors produces gray, whereas all the colors of light result in white.

There are many systems of classifying and arranging colors. A simple method is based on the three primary colors, *not a product of mixture:* red, yellow and blue. From various combinations of these all other colors are derived. These primary colors form a theoretical triangle with red at the top, yellow at the left, and blue at the right.

There are three secondary colors obtained by mixing one primary color with another. These have definitely accepted names: orange, violet and green. Red plus yellow equals orange. Red plus blue equals violet. Blue plus yellow equals green.

The secondary colors also form a triangle but opposite in direction from the primary triangle, and the

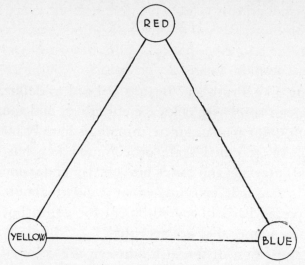

two triangles together form a star. Now mix each color with its adjacent color and we have the intermediates,

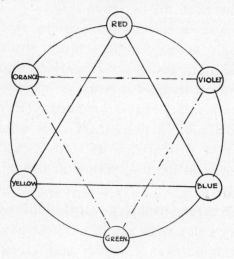

yellow green, blue green, blue violet, red violet. orange red, yellow orange.

We may keep up this process indefinitely, until we have a color circle—a circular rainbow of pure colors. Every spot in this circle is different from every other, and commercially and artistically they are given innumerable names so that it is quite impossible to establish a common language in colors. Therefore, it is important to realize that regardless of the name of the color, its components and its sources or bases are the determining factors.

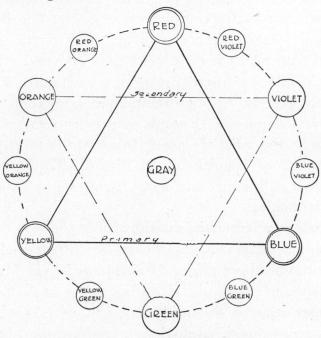

The Color Circle, as explained, is the equivalent of the Musical Scale. We must understand it, its sharps and flats, half tones and overtones before we may proceed intelligently to our harmonious composition of colors. That is a matter of nuances, accents and emphases, subtle gradations, distinctions of texture.

Each spot in the color circle is called a hue. It has a different wave-length from every other hue. Red is a hue, so is orange.

Besides mixing hues with each other we may mix them with white and obtain tints; we may mix them with black and obtain shades. It is common to refer to the degree of mixture of a hue with white or black as it value. Unmixed, its value is purity. Mixed, its value may be anything from a pale tint to a dark shade.

Each hue has its complement or contrasting hue— the point exactly opposite in the color circle—combined with which it produces a gray (theoretically).

Colors have a different relation to each other, which may be pleasant or unpleasant. A pleasant color relation is a harmony. An unpleasant color relation is a discord. And what we are trying to do is to arrange harmonies of color to avoid discord. This may be achieved with either analogous harmonies or contrasting harmonies.

Analogous harmonies consist of using several colors that adjoin or are close together on the chromatic circle. Such combinations can avoid monotony by varying the intensities of each color according to the area covered, stronger color for smaller areas.

Complementary harmonies, or contrast, use two opposites on the circle, i.e.: blue green, red orange. Quantitative analysis is even more important here; the colors being direct competitors, they will clash unless one is dominant. The dominance is principally a matter of area, but really good color schemes are based on the presence of the complement in the other color; this grays it and reducing its value, permits it to take second place.

The graying of colors opens wide the field of color harmony; the less positive the color the more colors can be associated with it.

There are certain principles which will aid in arriving at a satisfactory room composition in color.

Red and yellow are warm and advancing. Red is warmer than yellow. Blue is cold, receding.

Advancing colors seem to make things smaller. Receding colors seem to make things larger. A red wall will make a room seem smaller.

The secondary colors add the greatest contrast for their corresponding primary colors.

Contrasts are less pronounced with warm colors than with a warm and a cool color.

Shades and tints of the same color will go together.

THE PLANNING OF COLOR SCHEMES

There are three things to be considered in planning the color scheme of a room:

1. The use of the room.
2. The character of the room—its shape and exposure.
3. Personal likes and dislikes.

Bedrooms and living rooms are best when treated with quiet schemes, avoiding violent contrast or too much depth. Strong contrasts and vigorous colors are dramatic and will tend toward restlessness and lack of peace. In living rooms planned to be occupied over considerable periods the body tones—walls, floors and ceilings should be restrained and harmonious and some clear contrasts will enliven the room. Avoid muddy tone: taupes and dirty grays and washed out greens are dispiriting. Use clean colors.

Bedrooms come under the same warnings for restraint of strong color and the contrast is not so necessary. Even more than in the living room, keep away from muddy unclean color; let the colors be clean, light tones, and the actual hue is then only a matter of choice.

Libraries are preferably done in deep restful tones. Deeper colors close in a room; this is definitely a pleasing quality in a library, where a sense of space is less desirable than the feeling of retreat, shelter. Avoid active, large scale patterns or contrasts.

Dining rooms may be gaily or vigorously decorated as their usefulness is for short periods. A certain amount of brilliance is not out of place. Period rooms have their distinctive sets of colors and choice should be made largely out of the characteristic woods and materials. English mahogany is a vibrant tone against cream, gray green or blue walls; their values will depend on the size of the room and the exposure.

Avoid positive greens and reds if you wish to spare your guests at dinner. In any other room the wearers of clashing colors can move about and suffer quietly; in the dining room they are doomed to sit and feel like a permanent off note in a bad harmony.

Foyers and halls may utilize strong color and contrast at will. These are generally the most poorly lighted rooms and vigorous contrast defines lines and creates brightness.

Game rooms have little restraint other than personal ones. It seems better to leave the highest tones of gaiety to guests rather than to the walls, but this room has generally become the last retreat of mural excitement.

Nurseries should have bright, light colors which create sunlight effects.

As guest rooms will have a variety of occupants, they should be done in clear neutral colors rather than with excessive brightness or smartness.

The character of the room itself may rule out favorites or overcome prejudices. You cannot afford to use certain colors in certain rooms regardless of how you like them. The exposure to natural light is one factor. If the scheme is based on artificial illumination choose colors that respond to the tone of the electric light, but if the sun is a more important source, a different basis must be used. We are accustomed to considering north light as cold, south as warm, but we do not always consider the reflection from outside. Generally, this reflected color should be neutralized. Cold light can be modified with warm wall and ceiling colors. Avoid white ceilings and thin wall tones for cool exposures; yellow, tan buff, of clean tones, will make satisfactory walls. On south or warm exposures cool tones to any degree desired are good—blues, pearl grays, cool greens. Off-white walls are ideal for many rooms; the off quality may be changed by slight additions of colors to warm or cool the effect.

The shape of the room is most important when we understand the properties of different colors. Aggressive colors make rooms small, as those that are recessive make the walls appear less important and somehow further away. But the ceiling and floor must also be considered as planes of color. The same choice of light or dark, receding or aggressive, must be made for them.

Proportion of colors, once the basis of the walls is settled, will make or unmake your room. The large masses—sofas, draperies, large wood or painted pieces, increase contrast by their size. It is better to keep them in a restrained harmony with the walls, unless they are placed so as to dominate. The smaller objects may be more vigorously contrasted, but there must not be many of these contrasts or the effect will be spotty.

Bear in mind that wood is color, as well as fabric and wall paint or paper. So is metal; and so are other elements of the physical furnishings; and most of all, so is the light—natural or artificial.

White, perferable in an off tone, is a flexible, luminous background for many rooms. It is a foil for any color, best of all for clear ones.

Patterned fabrics or papers yield whole schemes in themselves. A strong design in a rug or drapery fabric may be the source of all the colors you need in a room. In such cases the proportion of color will become a matter for the most careful study.

1. Colors in large areas such as walls will look darker than they do in small samples.
2. Ceilings will look darker than walls of the same color.
3. Contrasts are best in poor light; in light rooms subdue the contrast; use analogous schemes.
4. Samples chosen in one light may look radically different in another light.

5. Names of colors in different materials are seldom the same and are often definitely misleading. Oil colors have one set of names, calcimine colors another; water colors a third; fabrics are always named whimsically; wood colors vary enormously. Only your eye can identify colors. It is better to see the color than to read a million words about it.

MIXING PAINTS

Wall paints are usually mixed by the addition of oil colors to white.

In mixing paints there are often several ways of arriving at colors that will vary only slightly in the final result. But the variation of cast will be enough to favor one combination over another. The component colors of a mixture are often good for the other color uses. For example; a buff wall may be painted with a mixture of white, burnt umber and turkey red. Fabrics of other color notes of either the turkey red shade or the umber color will be excellent with the buff.

The proportion of color added to the white makes all the difference in the world. You must watch the mixing and determine the proper shade or tint. All the following are based on the addition to white.

Biscuit   —Medium chrome yellow

Salmon Pink   —Medium chrome yellow, 1 part
Venetian red, 2 parts

Rose Taupe   —Medium chrome yellow, 1 part
Venetian red, 2 parts
Lampblack, 1 part

Amber   —Medium chrome yellow

Reed Green   —Medium chrome yellow, 4 parts
Medium chrome green, 1 part

Apricot	—French ochre
Tea Rose	—French ochre, 48 parts
	Venetian red, 1 part
Parchment	—French ochre, 3 parts
	Raw umber, 1 part
Sand	—Raw umber
Fawn Gray	—Raw umber
Chalk Blue	—Lampblack
	Prussian blue
	Medium chrome green
Nile Green	—Light chrome yellow
Aqua Green	—Medium chrome green
Buff	—Raw Italian sienna
Ivory	—Medium chrome yellow
Empire Green	—Dark chrome green
Louis XVI Blue	—Cobalt blue
Hydrangea Blue	—Cobalt blue
	Rose madder
Dusty Pink	—Rose madder
Pistachio	—Chromium oxide
Lemon Yellow	—Light or lemon chrome yellow
Colonial Blue	—Lampblack
	Prussian blue
Oyster White	—Ultramarine
	Medium chrome
	Turkey red
Pearl Gray	—Cobalt blue
	Lampblack
	Touch of yellow

CHAPTER XXI

LIGHTING

It should be unnecessary to make the point that the object of lamps and lighting is to reproduce daylight. However, the tendency to make lamps primarily a decorative feature has detracted in many cases from their value in illuminating a room. We will begin with the lighting in which the source of light is the least conscious, and progress to the most decorative form, or the independent lamp.

Formerly these two were merged, because there was no way of making light anything but a point, as a candle or lamp. These were essentially single points of brilliance which radiated more or less, and a room was lighted generally or spottily in proportion to the number of lights

The central lighting fixture was the 17th century contribution to diffused lighting. A great many candles hung in the middle of a room on a tremendous fixture and solved the problem beautifully—for the 17th century. We took the fixture and variously equipped it with candles, oil lamps, gas lights, and electric light bulbs. But the chandelier as such must be considered first an object of beauty and only secondly a design for lighting.

The wall bracket is similarly the child of the metal or glass sconce designed to hold a candle, oil lamp or gas jet on the wall without letting the heat damage the wall surface. As a source of illumination it is less efficient than the central fixture, and brings the light to a plane where it is least desirable. The center of the room is more the center of man's activity than the walls. The detached lamp is an infinitely better solution because it is portable to some degree, and its position as a source of light may be dictated by its relation to chairs, desks, etc.

Since such a light in the center of a room recreates the whole picture of the room, and in itself becomes the focal attraction to the eye, it has become customary to make these lamps highly ornamental affairs. Very often, the ornamental aspect has been in sadly inverse proportion to the lighting value. Nevertheless, lamps will continue to take a more and more important part in decoration, and it is not uncommon to find houses to-day equipped with no other lighting provision than outlets for lamps. The character of the lamp can be very well adapted to the style of the room. There are in historic periods so many minor objects of agreeable shape, form and texture, that will cheerfully accept conversion to torch bearers, that we need never go hungry for motifs for lamp bases. All the metals, pottery and glass, wood and paper, are suitable lamp base materials.

Shades should be studied primarily for shape. In traditional rooms, the shade is usually considered first in its shape and proportion to the base, rather than its efficiency in distributing light over the desired area. In a modern lamp we haven't even the excuse of making the lamp integrally beautiful, and if a modern lamp doesn't give good light it is definitely bad.

The shade may be of textile or any material that permits the desired translucency. It must be effective in screening the shape and in directing the concentrated light to the proper point. The spots of light in an otherwise darkened room have a way of producing highly dramatic centers of interest. Indeed, in stage setting the lighting is of the utmost importance. Every chair or group of chairs should be given some well considered source of light, or it fails of its purpose in organizing a group.

Lamps divide themselves roughly into floor lamps and table lamps. The floor lamp to-day tends to be distinctly unobtrusive for any period room, instead of the ponderous torchere bases and Roman candelabra of a generation ago. Floor lamps should be light enough to be easily portable, but firm and heavy enough to stand solidly.

The number and location of outlets is a very important factor in avoiding the possibility of a handsome composition being marred by straggling wires, to say nothing of the hazard of tripping.

Table lamps are now usurping much of the lighting formerly performed by floor lamps, and are more and more specialized. We have very large and important center lamps that require an architectural base in the form of an important table. We have lamps that are to be used in pairs flanking sofas or beside beds. Dressing table lamps are likewise used in pairs, and they permit the concentration of light. Desk lamps similarly restrict the light to a very small area, generally by having an adjustable shade of a non-transparent material, and a multitude of specialized lights of more or less appropriate decorative forms and materials.

In choosing and integrating the elements of light that we use in a room, it might be well to bear in mind that the most desirable lighting is always one that limits the area of intense light and enlarges the area of general light. That is to say that it isn't good to have a brilliant lamp in a dark room. If you are reading in a chair under a brilliant lamp, you will be absolutely blind to the rest of the room, and if you look up from the book the adjustment that you have to make is really a great strain. Therefore, in a living room or a library, or a room in which you read or work at a desk or at a piano, the best lighting is soft diffusion over the whole room, and a concentrated amount of light upon the immediate object of the eyes' attention.

In a dining room, the first consideration should be for the center of the table. The soft general lighting should be the area around the focal center of the room.

All indirect lighting must begin at the point that the light must emerge from a point above the average eye level, as the source of light is more powerful than the ordinary lamp and therefore distinctly irritating. This should particularly be remembered regarding indirect table lamps.

In adapting indirect lighting to period or stylized fixtures, the somewhat upsetting dramatic effect of having light flow from an unaccustomed object should not be ignored. The sticklers for tradition who would not put flowers in a Sheraton knife box may sometimes be found guilty of letting light emerge from such an object or from the top of a column or a cornucopia, or some other unusual source.

In many rooms it is desirable to approach the problem of lighting with some effort to reproduce daylight as nearly as possible, although in a lesser degree the general illumination of a room should partake of this character while the spot lighting should be conspicuously and genuinely artificial. Individual room lighting will be studied in the analysis of the various types of rooms.

ARCHITECTURAL LIGHTING

In electricity we have a new convenience in the form of the diffusion of light from a concealed source. This might be called architectural lighting in that it must be planned from the beginning of a room, or introduced through the use of structural members or surfaces. The source of the light must be invisible; the lighting comes from planes and surfaces which reflect light hidden in coves or recesses. These luminous surfaces may either be walls or ceilings, and the area of diffusion as well as the intensity of the light (the amount of light thrown upon the reflecting surface) may vary at will.

The lighting for such purposes is some form of strip lighting. The tubular shapes yield the best diffusion, and the lumiline bulb has been very extensively employed. Lumiline is an incandescent filament lamp; the newest development is the fluorescent type, a cool, highly effective unit. Color variations for various purposes are being studied extensively.

Indirect or diffused light alone is not entirely satisfactory in residence lighting. Such light provides a good general light but unless the overall intensity is uncomfortably great, there will be insufficient light at such specific points as centers for reading, desk surfaces, sewing, etc. We must continue to rely on lamps for such specific lighting; fortunately there are excellently designed lamps for all such purposes, ranging from the straightforward functional designs to the inherited ornamental forms.

Built-in diffused lighting may take advantage of beams, suspended or "furred" ceilings, and structural projections. A good method is to try to place the source in a location approximating the source of the natural light, such as the upper surfaces near windows. A secondary tool in the lighting problem is the use of mirrors judiciously placed. These will not only enlarge a room, but trap and multiply light, enliven dark spaces, and emphasize bright ones. Extreme care should be used, where mirrors are a considerable feature, to avoid the unpleasant repetition of artificial light spots through the reflection of lamps which will create an extremely confusing image and will tend to destroy rather than enhance a composition, to say nothing of one's physical comfort.

There is no doubt that theoretical and scientific lighting is beginning to emerge from its cocoon, and it may not be an overstatement to say that one of the greatest developments of the room in the next decade will be in the direction of artificial lighting.

CHAPTER XXII

WINDOWS AND WINDOW TREATMENT

Windows give us light, ventilation, protection, and vistas. Looking over the methods of treating windows that have come and gone leaves one with a suspicion that, in almost every period at least one of these points was overlooked. It follows that whatever the window treatment is, there must be some provision for changing it according to the varying demands of these four fundamentals. The means to this end have been shades, shutters, blinds, Venetian blinds, portieres, curtains, draperies and overdrapes, and these carry with them a whole system of dodges and subterfuges.

For the ordinary needs to-day a window should be permitted to do the following things: first, let in light that may be controlled as to both quantity and quality; second, let in light without air and vice versa; third, determine the degree to which the elements shall be admitted; fourth, let in air and keep out rain; fifth, allow for privacy.

Windows are of paramount importance because they contribute one of the dramatic elements to a room— that of light with all its subtleties and modifications.

The window then may be regarded as both a mechanical contrivance for the admission of light and air and a point of emphasis in the wall. Predominantly, the mechanical feature is our first consideration, and while the decorative aspect may be stressed as far as desired, it should never impair the primary reason for being. Simple as this sounds, it would have the effect, if administered literally, of banishing a very large number of very handsome window concoctions.

The question of ventilation, vistas and protection may be omitted from this work, but the value of the gradations of light in the creation of a handsome picture cannot be overestimated. These gradations are obtainable through the use of various forms of draping and other window treatment that form the basis of this section.

The architectural drapery may be divided into two classes: first, that which takes the window as an architectural frame and enhances it by means of more or less elaborately designed framings of fabric and other materials. The second method treats the wall itself as the frame of the window and will seek to admit the greatest possible light space under one condition, with the enlargement of this wall for the reduction of this light space. This will be achieved by the method of draping the *wall*.

In the first classification we must accept the architectural window, sometimes ornamented with pilasters or colonnettes, with pediments or architectural motifs. In such cases, all drapery must come within the lines of these motifs, or be framed by them. Where the architectural motif is less important the drapery will provide it, and will assume a definite form of its own which encloses the light area.

In the treatment of draperies by historical styles, we find a highly decorative type characteristic of each era, always growing out of the architectural characteristics that accompanied the interior. In the Elizabethan interior, for example, a great area of glass was required both for scale and to admit sufficient light into the large rooms. The light being generally gray and weak, every effort was made to maintain the value of all the available window space, so that practically all drapery of this period was made to draw completely back of the casing. There were no decorative cornices as the window reveals were deep enough to accommodate all the fabric and its operation.

Later periods exhibit more the Italian and French tendencies to impose great billowing masses of swagged and valanced fabrics. Chippendale draperies were designed in the most ornate architectural style, with extremely decorative cornices of wood and metal and elaborately gathered over-curtains. Draperies of such elaborate characteristics will have lighter weight materials of rather smooth finish. These styles will be found more emphatically true of the more feminine approach such as characterized the Louis XV and Louis XVI and the Directoire styles of France, the late 18th Century work of Italy, and the earlier Victorian forms and the Adam and other late 18th Century forms of England.

In current work, windows with architectural pretense are draped simply, within the frame. Windows lacking distinction architecturally may make up for this lack by highly decorative framing of the light space.

Contemporary rooms will vary highly with the particular derivation of the style. Forms deriving from classic treatment will use with some safety tie-back curtains and distinctive valances. The more functional and direct solutions will avoid the consciousness of window draping, and will attempt to conserve the light-yielding value of the window by draping the wall.

Some device for tying several windows together is often employed, such as predominant ceiling line or sill line, effected by minor reconstruction, with curtains covering the wall entirely around the window, from ceiling to floor, and capable of being drawn entirely across the windows. Modern rooms may very well rely on the great bank of fabric so produced for one of the most valuable effects at its disposal.

The use of under-curtains, blinds and shades will likewise be considered with relation to the entire style of the room, as well as the exterior aspect presented by these devices. It is generally desirable to carry the same shade effect through all the windows appearing on the same facade of a house. Sometimes this is apt to cramp our palette for some rooms.

One point that should be borne in mind in handling these devices, is to have them correspond to some degree with the wall color. They should not be treated as gaps in the wall. At night, the psychological effect of a black window is distinctly a bad one. One desires shelter, and the subconscious feeling demands the shutting out of this blackness. The quality established by shades or Venetian blinds should be one to make the wall more continuous over the gaps.

Venetian blinds in themselves are particularly desirable in that they are probably one of the best means of admitting light and ventilation with privacy as desired. They may also admit varying degrees of growing light or half light which is extremely picturesque.

Glass curtains accomplish the same ends, and in some rooms will permit the elimination of any other drapery, providing they are accompanied by some means of shutting out light as desired. We have, in the degrees of fineness for curtain fabrics, silk gauzes, voiles, swiss, cellophane weave, cellophane and chenille combinations, various combinations of light yarns of wool and cotton, nets varying from minute openings to coarse strong fishnet.

The color and quality of light may be vastly altered by the window treatment. Venetian blinds in themselves have a way of reflecting light modified in color by the color of the blind. Likewise, a net, gauze or a voile will throw a distinct colored light over a room, and do much to modify a sometimes undesirable lighting color. For instance, a north light that is cold and gray, can be made bright and sunny by using tones of yellow, orange or rose; while the too intense south or east exposure can be remedied with blues, blue grays, grays, and similar cool tints. It should be borne in mind that most of the light received in a room is a light of reflection rather than direct rays.

The vistas from the windows must be accepted as a very decided factor in the technique of draping. A room with a fine view should have nothing to spoil its enjoyment. The draperies should be transparent or capable of being withdrawn entirely. A definitely poor view should be obscured, rather than dominate. Sometimes it is even desirable to replace the windows presenting such a poor outlook with either frosted or translucent glass to eliminate the picture. Venetian blinds often serve this purpose very simply by admitting the light without the view.

CHAPTER XXIII

FURNITURE AND HOW TO BUY IT

For prince or pauper there is the inevitable beginning—how much to spend and how to get the most out of it. The budget consideration is so vital that the allotment of money for various divisions of furnishing and its most intelligent application should be considered before any definite move is made. Determine with all honesty what your real limits are before you begin, or you may find yourself skimping on one detail only to splurge later with less justification. Allowance must be made in the beginning for everything: furniture, floor coverings, window treatment, lamps and lighting, accessories. As there is an irreducible minimum to the cost of good material it would be better to limit the number of articles rather than to sacrifice quality.

It is equally true that above a given price you no longer buy better quality, but more detailed style, design, or limited production.

There is absolutely no general rule that will prescribe the percentages of decorating expenditure to annual income, rental paid, or any other fiduciary factor. Actually, the best method is to take the figure that you think should represent your maximum, detail it by rooms and then go out and see what the market affords. If you are doing your own buying, it would be advisable to furnish your rooms entirely on paper before placing a single order. If a professional interior decorator is spending your money for you, the chances are that he will be able to help you allocate the various expenditures before any conclusive plans are made. In either case, do not base final decisions on the basis of advertising matter alone, since price ranges are meaningful only in the light of the actual material.

When you sally forth, finally, you will need the wisdom of a Solomon to distinguish between the various claims and counterclaims. Since there are no set rules as to the construction or material of furniture, you will hear the same arguments being offered for and against. The conclusion is that you must buy very largely on faith and the reputation of the seller will probably be the most reliable guide. Of course, even the best stores sell the products of a variety of factories in order to cater to more than one price field. You must, therefore, accept as a second condition, having established the general price character of the store, the fact that you get about as much as you pay for. In the long run, there are no bargains and there is no Santa Claus. The house furnished exclusively with bargains, wholesale purchases, and special offerings will inevitably be an assemblage of odds and ends, unplanned compromises, and manufacturers' indiscretions.

The details we propose to give you as criteria, as well as salesmen's claims, may be open to contradiction or questions in individual cases, but insofar as they represent established practice on the part of many good manufacturers and have withstood much average use and abuse, they may be helpful.

First, wood must be recognized as an organic material. Even with the most perfect seasoning and selection it still may react in some way to variations in the moisture content of the air. You cannot detect in any furniture whether or not the wood has been properly seasoned, but you can expect that certain woods will exhibit less pronounced reactions than others. Walnut and mahogany are perhaps first on the list of cabinet woods. Successively after that we may place oak, maple, birch, gumwood, magnolia and pine. Most other woods will occur as veneers, in which case the strength of the core and the method of making are the vital factors. There are places in which the solid wood is best structurally. And there are others where nothing but veneer panels should be used, and you may most safely depend on the specifications of a reliable manufacturer.

Glue is a primary substance in the manufacture of furniture to-day, and to say "just glued together" is to indicate a comprehensive ignorance of the process of furniture making. Glues for every purpose, whether veneering, surface or end joining, have been given tremendous technical research, so that to-day's furniture may be said to be fundamentally a matter of glueing. The proper and sufficient use of the various glues creates joints that are actually stronger than the wood itself. A properly made glue joint will hold although the wood around it will break in the fibres. Most glueing is done with hot glue and warm wood. Clamping squeezes out the excess of glue and makes the joint tight. Of course, the best glueing will not atone for incorrect cutting and the precision of machine work in this respect is infinitely preferable to the work of the human hand.

The making of cabinets, chests, or the classification known to cabinet makers as case work, exhibits the most demanding artisanship. In examining the case, see how well drawers and doors operate, and how close the fitting is. On most mechanically produced furniture a center drawer guide is a valuable feature, although on hand-made, custom furniture, in which each drawer is fitted individually, they are rarely used. A dust proof panel between each drawer is very desirable. The drawer itself should be dovetailed at the corners, although with some designs this is not possible. The bottom of the drawer should be a three-ply panel. The material of the drawer sides and the general finish of this feature is a fairly safe index to the quality of the piece. In fine work mahogany or oak will be used for drawer sides. Successively less expensive work will utilize birch, maple, gumwood, poplar and basswood. A fine chest of drawers or cupboard will be reasonably firm, while an improperly designed or poorly built piece will accommodate itself so much to the shape of the floor as to make drawers and doors fit badly. This latter fact is a matter of degree, as practically every case will exhibit some tendency to twist unless it is built impossibly heavily. The slight variations in the floor can be corrected with tiny wedges when the piece is placed in its proper position in its room. See if the inside of the drawer is deep enough. A common flaw in lower priced chests is to have drawers shallower than the actual chest.

In some styles to-day, features like exposed pegging are being made much of. This is purely decorative (*sic*) feature, and even if it were actually a serviceable peg its being exposed would add nothing to its strength. Practically all furniture is joined by means of dowels or concealed pegs, or the mortise and tenon method. There may be so much good or bad in joining, according to the actual workmanship, that it is beyond the province of the layman to criticize this feature intelligently.

The construction of wood chairs is very particularly a product of design. A chair represents the greatest engineering achievement of the furniture designer, as it is subject to the most stresses and demands. It is our common practice to abuse a chair in every conceivable way, and there is no way of making a chair proof against most of this. The ordinary side chair, if it must be designed against tipping back, must have a stretcher or system of stretchers near the foot. Those styles, such as the Hepplewhite, Directoire and many modern forms that prefer to get along without stretchers, simply must not be tilted. Generally a wood seat chair is stronger than one with an upholstered seat. The Windsor chair and Chippendale's Chinese versions are among the best structural designs ever produced. The more extravagantly curved the leg of the chair, the greater its likelihood of breaking, as the wood grain runs in a fairly straight line, and it is along this line that the strain is borne. As woods tend to cleave along the grain, a chair leg which does not exhibit a continuous grain stands a very good chance of snapping. Strong corner blocks, where visible, will be an index to the strength of such a chair at the joints.

Upholstery and upholstered chairs are the blindest productions of the furniture maker. The recognition of this fact has led to extensive state legislation toward compulsory, explicit labelling of the inside materials of such chairs. The wood framework of an upholstered chair is best made of white ash, birch, maple and hickory. Somewhat less desirable are soft maple, gum, poplar, basswood, and pine. It is essential that these frames should be strongly glued, dowelled and fitted with corner blocks, never nailed together. This forms the framework for the webbing, springs, twine, burlap, cotton, and muslin that form the basis of the upholstering, and which you don't actually see and must therefore accept. The variety of individual possibilities in each of these materials is tremendous, and the use of any of them may be justified, so that it is useless to go into considerable detail here. A properly upholstered chair will have closely interlaced webbing, sufficiently and tightly tacked; the springs will be sewed down and tied frequently enough with a good twine. But since you can't shop for furniture with a penknife, you will accept the responsibility of the maker.

Loose cushions must be labelled as to contents in many states. Down, hair, springs, Kapok or cotton are the usual fillings. Down is the soft plumage next to the skin of birds and fowl. It is light, soft, and resilient, and is usually given consistency by the addition of a percentage of feathers. Goose feathers are the best; chicken feathers the cheapest. The percentage of the mixture determines the durability and resilience.

Hair may vary from the long stapled, curled fibres which were manes or tails of horses, through the various grades of cattle hair and hog hair, and the mixtures of these varieties. Hog hair is the shortest and least resilient, as it does not curl. The color of the hair has very little to do with the quality to-day.

Various kinds of springs used for the filling of cushions are serviceable and satisfactory, but are not used in the best work as they produce a comparatively stiff looking cushion. They are always used in conjunction with a padding material like cotton.

Kapok is a soft, silky, vegetable fibre imported principally from Java; very light in weight and very resilient, it has a tendency to break up into dust after considerable use.

Moss used for furniture stuffing grows in the South, and is used only in the least expensive furniture. It lacks permanent resiliency or staying qualities.

African fibre, palmetto fibre, coir fibre, tow and excelsior (wood wool) are offered as furniture filling in the less expensive qualities only.

Rubber has recently begun to play a great role in upholstering. A pre-formed cushion filler of a foamy rubber is extremely live, due to the molded-in air spaces which produce the greatest resiliency with least possible weight. An older product is a compound of latex and cattle hair which forms a spongy mass, resilient and durable.

The actual covering of a chair is akin to tailoring, and must be judged in the same way. Fine seams, properly tight surfaces, and the matching of fabric will be clearly apparent to the critical eye. Inasmuch as all the details of upholstered furniture construction are essentially hand work, the standards of judgment that apply to such work are quite personal. The fitting of the cover of a fine chair may not necessarily increase its life, but if such features mean anything to you, you must be prepared to spend a sizable sum for a properly made chair or sofa. The exposed parts of upholstered chairs are generally made of fine woods—walnut, mahogany, maple, rosewood, etc., and may be ornamented by the use of carving, painting or veneering. Much carving described as hand work is really machine carving that has been touched up by hand. It does not condemn it to call it machine carving, as the degree and skill of the hand carving is the point that will make it good or bad.

The coverings of upholstered chairs are treated in another chapter, but it is well to point out here that the appropriateness of the fabric should be the first consideration. Light weight or thin fabrics on much used chairs are headed for disaster. Any fabric should always be applied over muslin. The edges should be upholstered soft, so as to protect the material from excessive friction.

Beds, from a structural point of view, depend only upon the joint between the rails and the head and foot boards. The joining mechanism must be tight and firm to avoid creaking and wobbling.

Tables in themselves are simple joinery, but the extension features involve mechanical ideas with consequent dangers. The simple pivot in which two hinged leaves open like a book will almost invariably expose the top leaf to warping. Draw-top tables likewise are difficult to keep flat, and a warped leaf makes operation difficult. The center opening type to which leaves are added is always safe, but demands storage room for the leaves. Types with self-contained leaves usually have such small leaves as to make them worthless. Dining tables with center pedestals must have spreading bases in order to stand firmly. These bases rob the diners of foot room. The ideal dining table is either of the type having a slim pedestal with wide spreading feet or one with four legs at the corners. The former were exquisitely studied by Sheraton and Duncan Phyfe; excellent four-legged tables with out-stretchers occur in the styles of Queen Anne, Hepplewhite, the Louis's and the Directoire.

The actual manufacture of furniture of even medium price quality is at a very high point; it is doubtful whether better or even equally good furniture was ever available before this age.

We have machines to thank for this, for the precision and excellence of machine work can never be approached by the human hand. Machine labor wherever known was enthusiastically used from earliest times. Completely hand made furniture is no more desirable than a hand made automobile. But the production of furniture, unlike other modern creations, is still basically a handicraft; the actual assembling of the machine cut pieces, the fitting and reconciling of the vagaries of wood demand that fine work be done by skilled hands. It is at this point that the cheaper qualities fall down; the machine contribution is good, but the hand labor element is skimped.

The actual finishing of furniture shows the greatest need for hand skill. We have been oddly unsuccessful in obtaining fine finishes by machinery; they invariably lack the wood quality and are hard and mechanical. Tedious hand rubbing alone produces a fine finish.

Wax, shellac, varnish and paint are used as formerly but we have new finishes synthetically produced which have special advantages. Most furniture today is finished with lacquer, a nitrocellulose product. It has nothing to do with Oriental Lacquer. After the usual preparation of filling and sanding of the wood, the lacquer is sprayed on and rubbed to the desired finish exactly like varnish. Its speed of finish is its special virtue, but it also may be made to be resistant to alcohol, heat and moisture. It should be borne in mind that all claims to the contrary notwithstanding, there is no finish known that cannot be damaged by these elements; their resistance is only a matter of degree.

Good furniture finishes always show the wood clearly; the surface is not opaque or gummy looking. The variations in colors of the same wood will often show clearly; in cheap work where fine selection of wood is not made, these inequalities are covered over with a more or less thick "glaze" which deadens the whole effect to achieve uniformity. Even in better furniture where the various pieces of wood are carefully selected and matched, the joining of the boards shows and is not objectionable.

The "antique" finishes depend entirely on the semi-opaque glaze which is wiped off more or less as highlights are desired. They are usually overdone; never so badly as in the maple finishes. The whole process of finishing maple is calculated to destroy the nature of the wood and to substitute imaginary mellowness.

Nothing in the making, materials or finish of furniture can provide entirely against abuse or neglect. Furniture will suffer near radiators or open windows or excessive or insufficient moisture. Intelligent, careful treatment will prolong the life and increase the beauty of fine furniture as well as your automobile or your clothing.

Choosing furniture for style or authenticity is a difficult procedure without knowledge. The only safe guide is the reputation of the maker. Even if he copies old things with the utmost literalness, there is still the finish, the softness of old edges and some almost invisible quality that baffles the copyist. A thousand guides to "what to look for" may not help as much as the critical opinion of someone who knows, who can tell at a glance. Lacking this you can only steep yourself in knowledge of the period that interests you, and see if the questioned article conveys the same spirit.

Look at mirrors especially critically. See if they give a clear undistorted reflection. Certain "shock" mirrors give wavy broken images. Good plate glass mirrors are not too expensive to be used in all but the poorest homes. The color of the glass will also have variations that may pass unnoticed in the store, but may change your complexion to a greenish blue when you have it home. Bubbles and spots are marks of inferior qualities, but it is never possible to get glass absolutely free of marks of this type or with no color tone whatever.

The undersides of table leaves, the backs of chests and mirrors, the insides of drawers should be satisfactorily finished.

PART III

THE PRINCIPLES OF DECORATION

CHAPTER XXIV

ROOM PLANNING AND ARRANGEMENT

THE ARCHITECTURE OF THE ROOM

The material presented heretofore in this book has been factual; a presentation of the ingredients available to the decorator and the methods of use that have evolved in other times and places. From this point, we endeavor to analyze the conditions with which you, as decorator, must cope. Such material must necessarily be opinion. Differences in opinion make for variety in rooms.

The room may be, and usually is, so personal an expression that laws and rules might only cramp a positive taste or confuse an uncertain one. The ensuing chapters do not attempt to formulate tables and graphs of room layouts and color schemes. They merely hope to present a logical method of analysis, suggesting the approach rather than the actual solution. For that, your own good taste alone will suffice.

Here are the ingredients and the proportions; put them together and season to taste.

Your architectural background consists of the six planes that bound your room: floor, ceiling, and four walls. The inside shape is the proportion of walls and ceilings. A perfectly hollow room may yield a sensation of pleasurable or disagreeable space; your analysis of it will be the surest guide to its decoration.

311

Window openings, doors, fireplaces and other features may be architecturally good or bad according to their size and spacing. The details of style are mere decoration. The primary quality of a room is proportion. In using period styles for modern rooms, this is one of the first snags encountered. Each style has its definite proportions which were quite practical when originally used but which very often do not fit a 20th century dwelling.

Architectural ornament of all types may be used to develop or correct the basic features. It is the *ornament* that is usually referred to as the background: columns and pilasters, panelling, moldings, arches, pediments, mantlepieces, overdoors and overmantels and the whole architectural vocabulary. These are the *trappings* of architecture, not its forms. We can not escape the ugly fact that in an apartment house the architecture of the room is a matter of beams and corner projections that harbor posts and ducts; doors in corners and windows any old way; rooms too long, with windows at the end, or ceilings too low, or too many doors. Even a complete house will suffer from mechanical exigencies.

You can correct these features in many ways, by simple building or by judicious balancing with objects. If your room is decorated in the modern manner you can even neglect them or go so far as to utilize them in your plan. Sometimes, in the latter case, effects of balance or separation are achieved through variations in the wall colors. Receding or advancing colors can do the work of actual physical building. A too disturbed ceiling or a broken up wall can be made to retreat by painting it with a recessive color, apart from the other walls. But unless this is handled with judgment and discretion, the effect may become bizarre. In all modern work these solutions are so new and striking that they will be criticized more than a bad period interpretation.

The traditional backgrounds that permit of some elaboration with architectural motifs need be limited only by expense. Given reasonable proportions, any room can be dressed up to the scenic illusion we want to create. Lacking the means, much can be accomplished by the studied arrangement of furniture, draperies, pictures and mirrors or any objects that arrest the eye and which can be placed in harmonious composition on the wall.

But the wall decoration is comparatively minor; the basic composition must be the utilitarian, or the grouping of the objects which rest on the floor. This is the *plan* or floor arrangement.

THE PLAN

The plan of any room is dictated by the use to which you will put it. The use will indicate the kinds of furniture, and the amount. Placing will be determined by the relation to such physical features as windows. Desks, reading chairs and game tables must have congenial light. Dining tables must have room around them for service. Such details need not be enumerated since they are common sense, but every article of furniture will have some limitations of this character imposed upon it.

In practice the best way to approach your room problem is to make a scale drawing of it; then cut out

separate scale plans of each piece of furniture you will
require and move them about on the plan until you find
a satisfactory arrangement considering comfort, traffic
and perspective. Then draw elevations of each wall,
related to the floor plan as sketched and bring the
furniture up to the walls. After that your problem is
composition, or the reconciliation of the planes.

The composition of the wall may also be called the
pattern. Try to look at your room as through a frame.
You will find that in the picture of the chair against
the wall, the chair is not necessarily more important
than the wall behind it. Imagine a number of objects
cutting shapes out of the flatness of the wall; imagine
them not only as light and shade, dark and light, but
with colors that have in themselves the qualities of
aggressiveness, recession, interest or antagonism,
warmth or cold. The whole visual picture is the basis
of composition.

We compose in color and texture as well as in mass
and line. You can use color to modify your composition; it will narrow or widen your walls or lower your
ceiling or make balances of unsymmetrical spaces.
Large masses or surfaces of negative color can be balanced by small bits of sharp aggressive color. Whether
by color or actual mass, this subtle balance is called
Occult. It has always been used skillfully by the Orien-
tals. The classic western conception of repose is symmetry.

In contemporary designing there is often this effort
at balancing things unevenly. The modern designer ac-
cepts the fact that the objects needed in a room rarely
come in pairs. He does not feel justified in forcing one

object into the shape of another in order to obtain balance. Since he has no cliché about dividing a room into two instead of the conventional three parts, he will work out some split, and through the use of colors and masses of distinctly varying proportions, may obtain nice balance, apparently unself-conscious.

The furniture used in modern decoration is also very often designed unsymmetrically. When planned for a purpose, or where the function of the piece is improved by it, it is acceptable, but unsymmetrical shapes used only for novelty are in danger of growing tiresome. Dressing tables, chests of drawers, desks have been composed in step-down levels. On the whole it is likely that these unsymmetrical pieces wear out, aesthetically, faster than the symmetrical. It may be that because of human physiology, we accept symmetry as a basis of design.

Occult or symmetrical, you will strive for balance in every particular. Balance the patterns and textures of fabrics used in chairs and draperies and rugs; balance the outline and relative weights of pieces of furniture. This last is called scale: it is the proper proportion of one thing to another, as a table to a chair, or a chair to a wall space.

The primary rule in combining furniture of various periods is to study the scale. Each style has its characteristic scale; Hepplewhite is fine, as is Louis XVI; Louis XIV is large. Therefore Hepplewhite mixes with Louis XVI but not with Louis XIV. With modern furniture particularly one must conquer the desire for tremendous easy chairs in small rooms before a satisfying composition can be obtained. Whatever your style, be sure that the furniture you buy is in scale with the room.

Ways to achieve scale in a room are many. For instance, you can begin by making the surfaces of the room more dominant—that is to say, iron out the walls. Let us suppose that we have a room with three windows at one end, badly arranged so that they leave small spaces. You can flatten out that whole finicky wall by draping it as a mass. Take several thicknesses of net or some material that won't obstruct your light and drape the entire wall, and it will take on a kind of unity that makes it one element instead of six or seven, as would be the case were each window allowed to express itself. All-over carpeting again simplifies the design of the floor as an element. Thus, having obtained a complete surface, you have a larger foil for a bulky chair or whatever object is to go in front of this large wall. If, on the other hand, the objects that you have are spindly, thin or too small, find some way of dividing the background so that each object has its place within the frame. It does not follow necessarily that you will achieve this scale with form alone. Color may upset the whole notion of scale by reversing the procedure.

Bookcases are serviceable in solving problems in scale composition or background. They have no prescribed shape, they are comparatively flat, and they yield an interesting human surface when filled with books. They may be high where height is needed or may be long low lines, to underscore or emphasize a composition. In period work they become architectural in decoration; in modern rooms they can convey a picture of pure line or abstract bulk.

CHAPTER XXV

ROOMS

In the organization of a room, the first consideration is *what* is the room for and, second, *who* is going to use it? The elementary room of the earliest historic houses or of the simplest living conditions to-day is an all-purpose room in which the occupant sleeps and works, rests and sees his friends, takes his meals and his leisure. In the primitive house such as the New England colonists erected in that cold winter of 1620, a single bare room was a satisfactory scene because it accomplished shelter, when that was the most urgent need.

But with the growing enrichment of life and the ascendancy of the individual came the division of the house into specialized rooms, just as with greater wealth to-day comes the need for a larger house or apartment, with its various specialized parts. The progress of this specialization has developed an infinity of clichés about furnishing these various rooms, and in the succeeding paragraphs we will attempt to break down the fundamental needs of each type of room and the best approach to their provision and organization.

The room or rooms must serve primarily the following purposes: sleeping, eating, bathing, preparation of meals, reading, study, rest and relaxation, entertainment of friends, reception, storage, and provision for children, guests, invalids, and other persons not partaking of the common activities.

FOYER OR ENTRY-HALL

The approach to the living room through whatever vestibule, foyer, hall or whatever may be the anteroom, should be comparatively undecorated, hospitable without being too relaxing. It therefore becomes formal and comparatively sparsely furnished, containing only such functional pieces as will facilitate reception and the changing from or to outdoor clothing. This, of course, includes mirrors as an important factor, a seat and table of some unimportant kind, and a closet or other means of storage. A set composition of console, whether table, chest or low cabinet, should have a mirror over it; the composition may be extended with side chairs, etc. The size and pretentiousness of this anteroom will vary with the size of the living room it serves, and should be a consistent approach in style and color suggestion. The floor material should be more serviceable, such as tile, rubber, linoleum, or bare wood. Wall treatment should be reserved and formal.

FUNCTION OF LIVING ROOMS

The living room as the central theme in man's daily activity must be considered first as a room from which all the specialized activities stem. It is a strange commentary on Victorian life that until thirty years ago living rooms as such did not exist. There were dining rooms, parlors, perhaps drawing rooms in some more formal homes, libraries, studies, dens, and at times rooms called sitting rooms, but nothing specifically called a living room.

The return of the living room marked a return to sanity of function and to-day this is the first room of any house or apartment. It is a return to the function of the Great Hall of the early English house, in which people lived, ate, talked, danced, slept, fought and loved.

It is into the living room that we take our guests and visitors, and it is primarily by the living room and its decoration that they judge us and our standard of home living, before we admit them to the intimacy of a meal with us in the dining room or make them house guests for a night in the guest bedroom. It is our interior front, more exposed to the judgment of our friends and the rest of the social world than all the rest of the house put together.

The living room presents the widest range of individual specialization or the lack of it. It varies in formality from the set picture devoted only to the entertainment of callers (the drawing room), to the opposite extreme of informality (the sitting room-study-recreation room, with possibly one end reserved for dining and even some provision for the occasional accommodation of an overnight guest). The formal living room will presuppose the existence of more intimate rooms in which the individual may relax for reading or study. It is a room in which all the specialized individual activities have found space elsewhere, while the completely informal room comprises all the daily activities of the occupant.

THE FORMAL LIVING ROOM OR DRAWING ROOM

As the primary consideration of the formal living room is the entertainment of guests, there will be, first, chairs in number and style planned to dispose of people in harmonious groups. No one need sit alone because of the inept isolation of a chair. The sociable grouping of two or more seats is the soul of this room, whether it centers about a fireplace, a window, a piano, or a table.

Take into account the fact that people will tend to break into groups. It is hard to get more than five to sit in a group unless they are overwhelmed by one central figure (who may ultimately become a bore). In any case, the planning of chairs should be such that the group may enlarge or break up at will. This will prescribe fairly portable chairs, and it is to be noted that the periods which represent the greatest height of social intercourse developed chairs of precisely this type. 18th Century England and France, where good talk flourished, and where extensive social interplay is one of the outstanding characteristics, are noted for the variety and comfort of their light chairs. In such rooms the great easy chair for reading and dozing is out of place.

The grouping of these chairs will follow an organized architectural scheme, with dominant points emphasized as being more desirable to sit in. The group around the fireplace, or the arrangement of chairs with relation to a window, will inevitably set up certain balances. The variety of styles of chairs is not nearly as important as the things that hold them together. The fireplace group is automatically linked by the fire,

DINING ROOM OF BRANDON, PRINCE GEORGE CO., VIRGINIA IN THE GRAND MANNER
OF THE LAST YEARS OF THE 18th CENTURY.

Courtesy William Helburn, Inc.

NEW ENGLAND DINING ROOMS FEATURED CORNER CUPBOARDS FOR THE DISPLAY
OF CHINA, SILVER, ETC. PINE CUPBOARD LATE 18th CENTURY.

Courtesy Henry Weil.

ALVAR AALTO.
Courtesy Artek-Paskoe.

COLLIER'S HOUSE OF
IDEAS.

Edward Stone, Architect.
Dan Cooper, Decorator.

Randt Photo.

ROBSJOHN-GIBBINGS.

BALANCE THROUGH SYMMETRY.

Margery Sill Wickware,
Decorator.

ROOM FOR A SMALL BOY.
Joseph Aronson, Designer.
Drix Duryea Photographs.

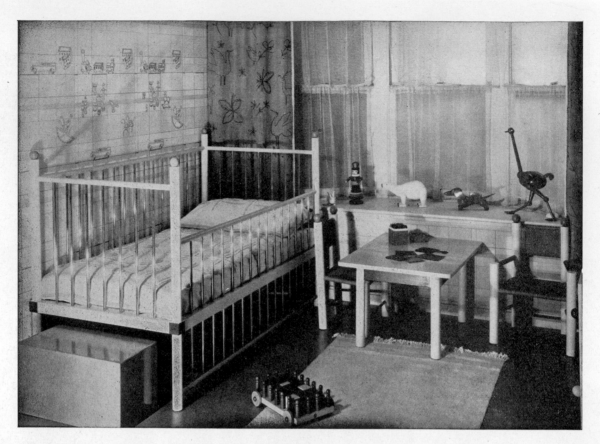

NURSERY AND JUVENILE FURNITURE
By Ilonka Karasz.

Courtesy "Decorator's Digest."

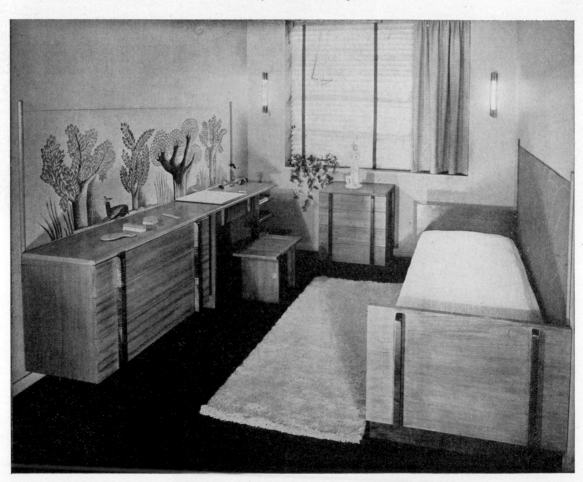

PARENTS' RETREAT.

William Muschenheim.

EUGENE SCHOEN, Architect.

whereas a group in another corner opposite may center itself about an important table. The lighting, whether through lamps or windows or both, will serve as the marker for each of these groups. The lighting of the whole room cannot depend upon the special lighting of each group; there must be some general lighting which should be bright without glare.

As formal entertainment will sometimes feature such rooms, the means of this entertainment, as music, might provide a characteristic center for the disposition of chairs or even of several groups.

The details of floor coverings and draping will, of course, follow the particular historic style.

There would ordinarily be a consideration of the more festal aspects of entertainment, like dancing. The floor, therefore, on such occasions should be suitable for dancing, although on most occasions it would have a covering.

Carpets or large rugs are the proper floor covering; fine Oriental rugs are at their best here. In fact, the whole effect should be the richest possible for the particular menage. The chairs may be covered in formal fabrics, silks, damasks and others whose durability may be second to their beauty.

The other pieces should not detract from the formality. Ornaments likewise should be impersonal, and should be objective rather than souvenir. Important pictures in good wall compositions may be centers of interest. Small pictures should be grouped; do not use personal photographs. The more formal the room, the more occasion there is for mirrors and similarly architectural compositions. The wall treatment, likewise, will be either plain or simple, or highly decorative, according to the style employed, or the degree of formality. The drawing rooms of small houses and apartments may emphasize the ornamental to a greater degree than would be true of the more intimate rooms, which permits more decisive color schemes.

LIVING ROOM

The living room that expresses a more generalized occupancy will have a certain number of possible groupings of chairs, but will also include distinctly easy chairs of the loungey type in which the individual may take his ease. Possibly a desk or work table, bookcases and cabinets for personal use; a sofa or divan which might even be a bed on occasion, and possibly provision for some sort of dining, with the incidental small chairs readily available. Such a room will be the catch-all for every activity the owner might require. It might include a piano, a permanent arrangement of table and chairs for games, phonograph or radio.

The wall treatment here will be more restful, or less ornamental. An all-over carpet with quiet or no design is preferable.

While the segregation of functions in such a room is apt to develop spots of interest, it should still be borne in mind that if entertainment is a factor it should be possible to make groups. No room is successful where it is not possible for a number of people to sit within easy communication of each other. In planning the arrangement of the groups, it is important not only to consider the grouping on the floor, but how it will appear against the wall.

The essential distinction of this type of all-purpose living room is that it may have grouping or lack of grouping at will. Where grouping is required, all chairs should be within access of one another. These should be planned in number and type to accommodate the average number of guests, and should be able to be disposed in a group or groups within the requirements of the owner.

The plan of such a room becomes necessarily informal, and will probably develop the separate functions in different parts of the room, based on such architectural features as a fireplace as a center for the seating group, an interesting window end which would provide light both for a desk or for several seatings, and the piano likewise within range of natural light.

Bookcases in such a room can be made to form a very useful architectural background, and there is no limit to the variety of forms that they may take. They may be made to flank the fireplace, if any, or may constitute in themselves a dominant feature on a large wall, whether through a long series of bookcases or an entire wall of books, or one of the classic forms of breakfront cases.

Almost every period will produce an inspiration for this type of architectural treatment, even though it may not have in actual fact a true prototype.

The treatment of walls and windows is better for being restrained, as this room will undoubtedly be occupied for a considerable proportion of the time and there is the consequent danger of a vivid color scheme becoming over-obtrusive and therefore boring. An ornamental feature can become a bore under these conditions, and magnificent drapery or highly patterned wall papers are not conducive to the restful comfortable atmosphere that such a room should provide.

The color schemes will derive from preference, based on exposure to natural lighting, the size of the room and the degree of intimacy that the owner wants to express. Light, unassertive walls are best.

A living room in a small country house is better with a neutral coloring, with lightly patterned fabrics. If the room is very large, the walls may be darker and somewhat positively colored. In no case should such a room be excessively warm or cold in color, or busy in pattern, because it is planned for occupancy in cold and warm weather, and one day's warmth of color may be another day's heat.

Carpeting contributes to the comfort of such a room in many ways, particularly in the absorption of sound. It may have color, but is better not too dark, as very dark shades show dirt too much. The lighting should be specialized so far as each particular function goes, the desk, piano and the game or dining table being provided with appropriate individual facilities, with provision for lighting each chair or group of chairs, as well as the over-all lighting.

Individual tables are needed to serve each chair. As some form of refreshment often accompanies entertainment in such rooms, each guest should be provided with a table or surface on which to set a glass, plate, or ashtray.

The individual will probably allow himself a wider range of expression in such a room in the matter of pictures and ornaments, and the decorator's province here is to see that they conform to a recognized plan of organization with relation to the furniture and the available wall spaces. There is no limit to the number of pictures that can be used, providing they are grouped intelligently and with an eye to composition. Ornaments, too, can be arranged at will, again with the limitation of keeping them under control as far as the outside form goes.

BEDROOM

The bed is obviously the major object in the bedroom. We have also come to associate the storage of clothing, dressing, etc., with the bedroom, although this need not be so. In the more specialized apartments a separate dressing room takes care of furniture for these other functions.

In the days of draughty rooms beds were built high to escape this discomfort. Since improved ventilation and heating have practically eliminated this evil the beds are designed with much less height.

The design of bedding now permits a much more compact, more comfortable unit. Since it is expedient to have a bed movable we mount it on rollers. A footboard may be necessary to cover the ends of blankets. Some persons may prefer to dispense with the footboard in order to make the room look larger but the individual's comfort should determine this detail as well as the position and type of beds. Headboards are invariably desirable practically, as a prop for pillows, and because they may be used as the center of the design of the room. Thus they provide a vertical plane to act as contrast to the decided horizontal plane which forms the bed. Harmonies in the materials grow out of this opposing set of planes. Consider the relation of the plane of the bed to the floor, the plane of the bed to the headboard, and the plane of the headboard to the wall behind it. The bed is preferred low on the theory that the fewer high things there are in the center of the room, the more open the room will appear. In other words, we do not cut up the air in the middle of the room; the lower the bed, the less space it will take. The tables will naturally be low enough to serve the beds properly, and should take as little space as possible.

To most people some provision in the way of light and side table is an essential part of the bed. Similarly, the relation of the telephone to the bed is one that cannot be ignored if we want to avoid the familiar tangle of telephone wire, light wires and the various other appurtenances that clutter up the side table. Breakfast in bed is a function that can be made more convenient by means of a properly planned table.

Unless this function is relegated to a separate room, there will be some provision for dressing. Here the primary object is a mirror, preferably large. This should be properly lighted, artificially as well as naturally. Moreover, there must be a convenient place for the storage of articles used in dressing: a table with drawers or a chest; and a seat of some kind.

The tendency is less and less to the display of objects used in dressing. Combs and brushes, atomizers and manicure accessories have no business cluttering up the top surfaces. They belong in drawers. The top surface is intended for certain work, and should be kept cleared for action. The surface should be one that is impervious to the attacks of perfumes, cosmetics and considerable wear. It should be low enough not to take up too much visual space, and high enough to enable one to go through all the motions without inconvenience.

The storage of clothing is an accepted function of the bedroom, unless it is taken care of elsewhere either in a properly equipped closet or in the previously mentioned dressing room. If it is in the bedroom, the piece of furniture for the purpose is one of a possible variety of chests of drawers. We have discarded the old notion of a tall chest for men and a low chest for women. Whichever type and shape best houses the required clothing is the best for the purpose, besides the matter of how it affects the design of the room. For men the drawers must be deep enough for shirts. This is not often true of commercial furniture. Most men have very set ideas about how they like their clothing disposed. In some instances shirts may be kept filed vertically, and it is perfectly conceivable that a piece of furniture might be designed on this basis. Similarly, there is no reason why the average man's requirements should not be considered in planning a chest of drawers to the extent of providing drawers deep enough to accommodate shirts, shallow drawers for the storage of collars, socks, etc., and deeper drawers for bulky things like sweaters.

On the other hand, women generally prefer shallower drawers and more of them, to avoid crushing and to take less space.

Recently much attention has been given to a better

arrangement of closets. These are larger now and very often designed with units of drawers, shelves, trays, etc., which will take all or part of the individual's clothing, in addition to the customary hanging space.

A chaise longue may be desirable for napping and resting, and of course this will require the incidentals of lighting and a small table, and its design will be guided by the same factors—comfort, proportion, spacing.

More and more people nowadays do not want dressing tables—they dress in the bathroom. In such cases it is desirable to have some kind of dressing table there. Most commonly the man uses the wash basin with the mirror above it. It is possible that some time a wash basin at table height will be marketed, growing out of this habit. Any table should permit the person dressing to approach close to the mirror with proper lighting. In lighting mirrors, it is the reflected object that must be illuminated, not the mirror. The glass may be entirely in the dark.

The color scheme of the bedroom must not depart from the initial purpose of the room: to conduce to repose. Clean, subdued tones will be best and the paint should be non-glistening, which does not reflect light harshly. Papers should avoid busy patterns that cram the walls and which may become intensely annoying. If pattern is desired, a plain or inconspicuous figured wall can be decorated with a narrow border pattern.

Lighting should be specialized at the bed and at the dressing table. A general light is good, preferably an inconspicuous centerpiece in the ceiling.

COMBINATION ROOMS

Many people think of the bedroom not as the boudoir, but as a combination sitting room and study. It is the most personal room, one's own room in which can be found seclusion and detachment, solitude and rest. Often such a room will reduce the bed to a glorified couch, and will emphasize other elements not heretofore stressed with the bedroom—desk, bookcases, or provision for social reception, chairs, radio, etc. We find this is particularly true of young people who have established somewhat independent social lives from that of their parents, and particularly want a room in which they can entertain their friends. Here the bed often becomes a sort of daybed or couch which is used for sitting and lounging as well. Several easy chairs and incidental tables, etc., complete the picture. Often this is an outgrowth of the college dormitory room which housed all these functions. Young people coming out of this atmosphere carry over the habit of using this all-purpose room as their own, and there find the privacy they require for their work, rest and entertainment.

From this it is an easy step to visualize the room which, while predominantly a living room, might also be used for sleeping. Such a room would have a couch which would be a comfortable seat for several people, as well as a bed. Of course it will also have other chairs and whatever additional furniture is indicated by the activities of the owner. Bookcases, if there are books, are better made too large for the present supply; a radio, which might be housed in the bookcase sections, worked into the walls in some way, or into an independent cabinet, a phonograph, as part of a combination with the radio, or as an independent unit.

The radio is preferably treated as an instrument and not as a piece of furniture. Whereas a piano has a definite shape indicated by its technical necessities, the radio can be compressed into such a variety of sizes and shapes that it adds an unnecessary unit to make it into an important case.

Chairs for the comfort of a group of people may or may not be lounge chairs. There should always be provision for those who do not like to sit in low, soft chairs. Older people often find the latter uncomfortable and will prefer one in which they may sit reasonably upright and which requires no effort to get out of. Such a chair will often be the "pull-up" type, a partially upholstered seat with an open frame. Many persons prefer to read in such a chair. Then again, some prefer to read at a table, and in a great many living rooms a center table of some kind will be found a distinct convenience. This should be about normal table height, should not provide interference to close sitting, should be large enough to leave some free space beside carrying the proper complement of smoking accessories or reading material of current interest, etc. A lamp for this group would either set directly on the table or be placed in conjunction to it on the floor.

The lounge chairs should be low and heavy and since they are not easily movable they should be supplemented by other chairs which are comparatively light.

There is a not altogether justified tendency to excessively heavy armchairs and sofas. These tend to disorganize the scale of a room. They take floor space out of proportion to their utility and they are not nearly as comfortable as they look.

There is no doubt that the more exaggerated forms of any style are the ones that go out of favor first. Chair buyers would do well to consider whether there is any real virtue in making chairs of unnecessary elephantine proportions. Anyone interested in having furniture that will endure in style and that will continue to be valuable should bear in mind that any unnecessary bulk, any extremity of design that does not further the direct purpose of the object, is an exaggeration; and these superfluities will outmode the article in a short time.

The table might on occasion be a card table, in which case there must be provision for seatings suitable for that purpose. This would be by means of light, smaller chairs; these chairs might either be of the folding type to be stored in a closet, or simple side chairs that would find other uses in the room on other occasions.

Another possibility would be to have this same table on occasion serve as a dining table in conjunction with these chairs. A desk might also be a feature of such a room. Since it is a room of considerable circulation, it would be advisable to have such a desk equipped with drawer space so that the user's papers may be kept with some privacy.

The lighting of such a room would be studied for provision for such specialized functions as well as general light. The individual chairs might in some cases be lighted by small standing lamps; an indirect-light fixture might illuminate one whole end of the room as a social unit, or the same unit might light the grouping used for dining or cards. For parties, where larger numbers of people are present and apt to circulate somewhat, a general all-over lighting is required, prefably through a central fixture with some indirect lighting.

DINING ROOM

In the organized house or apartment the probability is that the first function of the living room to be specialised would be that of the dining room. This room, of course, depends upon the table. The minimum and maximum number of persons to be seated at it determines its size. As it is just as uncomfortable for four people to sit around a table planned for twelve as the reverse, the table would necessarily have an expansion and contraction feature in which the expansion is based on each additional seating allowance of about 21 inches. In considering the size of the table allow at least three feet on all sides for the chairs, and for the passage of servants. An oval or round table is more flexible in this respect than an oblong table; but in any case the seating preferences of the hostess must be the entire basis of table planning. The base of the table should not be an obstacle to comfortable seating. Many pedestal types in modern styles are definitely objectionable.

The chairs should be comfortable but not too large, sufficiently high-backed to be comfortable to the average person, and covered in a material that anticipates the worst. The height of both table and chairs are rather sensitive dimensions, and regardless of style are not subject to much manipulation. An inch variation in the

height of a table is distinctly felt. In almost all periods
the height of dining tables has hardly varied between
29 and 30 inches, and a chair to correspond will have
a seat height of from 17 to 18 inches.

The sideboard or buffet will provide some storage
space and surface to aid in serving. The storage feature
is not so highly emphasized, as linens and silver can
be as satisfactorily closeted in the pantry and elsewhere.
The display feature of the sideboard has been constantly on the wane. While there is a certain decorative
value in some pieces, most of us recall only too clearly
the mound of cut glass and silver jiggers that made a
nightmare of the dining rooms of our youth. The
ancient custom of keeping certain liquors accessible to
the dining table bears out the usefulness of the buffet.
An independent serving table near the pantry door is
sometimes desirable, particularly where the dining
service assumes greater ceremony. In this case, a screen
will also be a valuable factor.

The lighting of the dining room is a particularly interesting point in that the center, or focus, of the dining
room is the center of the table. Proceeding radially
from this focal center of light it is better to keep the
walls dark so that the servants passing behind the diners
are not obtrusive. The central lighting over the dining
table is therefore the most desirable.

By the same token, brilliant mirrors on the walls are
likely to distract the guests. Mirrors as a table decoration should never be placed in such a way that guests
see themselves. People seeing themselves eating are apt
to be very self-conscious. The same is true of all table
decorations that in themselves attract too much atten-

tion, such as goldfish, or anything with action. Center-pieces should be low enough so that people can see each other comfortably across them. The dining table is the most sociable place in the world, and the decorations must not absorb any of the sociability.

LIBRARY

The library naturally is devoted only to books. A desk, easy chairs, satisfactory specialized lighting in the form of desk and reading lamps, tables of a height suitable for reading, end tables for smoking things, and a general air of quiet and monastic seclusion should characterize these rooms.

The flooring should be sound-absorbing, with carpets as first choice. Colors and patterns may not be aggressive; browns, tans and greens have been most successful. We have come to think of libraries as masculine rooms. Remember to provide more book space than is needed at once. There must be provision for large volumes and periodicals.

GUEST ROOMS

Guest rooms, of course, will be a trifle more general than the personal rooms, since you probably will want to adapt them to a variety of people. Certain little comforts that are sometimes overlooked are desirable—a luggage rack, for instance. The guest room should also partake a little bit of the living room, so that the guest has a place to which he may flee. Have an easy chair and a writing table: colorful bright tones are recommended, but avoid overdefinite shades which may be offensive.

NURSERY

Here people are sometimes inclined to be lavish out of proportion to the functions and character of the room. The child is so highly responsive to his environment as soon as he begins to notice things, that the objects he sees should be readily perceptible—that is, they should be simple forms to understand. Avoid complicated pieces and high decoration. A great deal of nursery decoration is really adult infantilism. To a child, what we call nursery figures are very often not amusing—just as the use of baby talk in speaking to a child is unnatural. We should not decorate his room with infantile grotesques because we think that is what he will draw. He will quit drawing those things just as soon as he can.

The essential furniture for the nursery will be, of course, the crib, or some bed provision, of which the primary essential is that the child can not fall out. Cribs should be designed so that children can not put their heads between the bars, or be poisoned by the paint.

The ends of cribs are best made solid, with the sides open enough to permit sufficient ventilation. The crib should be high enough to permit the child to be picked up easily, and deep enough to prevent him from climbing over the side. Large rubber tired rollers are desirable. The wood should be plain and hard; remember the tooth and toy marks. Paint finishes are best; particularly as they can be washed.

A utility table is essential for handling a very young child; let the top be of rubber or linoleum. There should be handy provision for all the appurtenances of baby tending, either in drawers or on wall shelves at the right height, handy to the work table.

Chests of drawers for children's clothing are often made so low that at an early age the child can reach his own things, which means that a child can be taught to put them away. Everything that it is permissible for the child to reach should be within his range. Chests for books and toys that the child uses in his playtime should be low so that the child will acquire the habit of orderliness in putting them back and the independence of getting the things he wants himself. There should be a low blackboard. A panel of cork, celotex or similar material permits the child to tack up pictures and drawings at will.

All parts of the furniture, walls, and floors should be easily cleaned; wood surfaces should be plain and washable. A few loose rugs, or one larger one, are best made of a hard woven material; cotton, wool, or linen with no pile. Above all, keep the floor area open.

There should be one general light, and a small light remote from the crib. Colors should be light, clear and gay, but not garish or too vigorous in large areas. Keep the nursery simple and uncluttered; preserve all possible floor space.

CHILD'S ROOM

The period when the child emerges from the nursery stage has been neglected. This is really the time when he uses furniture most because he begins to go to school. A desk is an important object. He is acquiring and crystallizing his habits of orderliness, developing a sense of possession, and the responsibilities that attach to it. For this stage, seek simplicity, ruggedness and a little smaller scale than would be true of adult furniture; also a youthful quality and directness of line.

MISCELLANEOUS ROOMS

The cellar room and attic room may be done in any manner, depending upon the use to which they will be put. They are so informal in their basic nature that there is considerable leeway in their decoration. If you want to paint stripes in one, make it look like the deck of a ship, or the Grand Canyon, no one will say you nay. In their very nature these rooms are informal, and the liberty of your action is limited only by your taste and purse.

For game rooms we would want comfortable chairs covered in very durable material. Portable, light chairs may be used here and there as possible combinations for different types of games. Of course, there will be arrangements for setting up additional tables. Surfaces should be able to withstand careless treatment of cigarettes, alcohol, foods and beverages. The bar is probably the most frequent and most useful adjunct of such a room, and will vary from a little cabinet for the storage of liquors which will have a resistant top suitable for the mixing, or will go to the extreme of an elaborate counter with back bar, mirrors, special lighting and shelving for glassware, etc., that approaches the professional bar in importance and cost. If it is along these lines it might be desirable to have high stools, as people like to perch near a bar. The top of the bar should be of a definitely resistant material or of a wood surface with an oil treated top.

Hangings and curtains in a playroom take into account the fact that some fabrics have a tendency to retain smoke and smells. Likewise the flooring material is best chosen of tile, rubber tile, rubber, linoleum, cork or wood. Incidentals to this type of room might be a ping pong table, or in a large house, a billiard room or bowling alley.

The kitchen is best when it is a good machine. The individual items that go into it are not in the decorator's province—they are in the engineer's field. Sink, stove, cupboards and icebox or refrigerators are all things that are being given so much technical attention to-day and there is nothing the decorator can say to improve on them. If you must have a color scheme in your kitchen, go ahead. The kitchen and the bathroom should really be regarded as factories. They are purely utilitarian. Their furnishings are objects of technical and scientific interest to which a great deal of thought has been given, and very successful things have been produced. A few years ago we were all over-enthusiastic on the subject of color. Every dishpan had to have a fancy tint. We painted roses on canisters. This is on the wane. We begin to have straightforward kitchens, with white, or a little clear color to take off the harshness. Bathrooms are a nice, clear, clean white tile, and rarely have paintings of monkeys and coconuts and palmtrees.

We have repeatedly mentioned Season to Taste. This is *your* special ingredient. Be free to use your own feeling about form and color; about everything in decoration, and the chances are that you will turn out a pretty good job. Providing, of course, you stop to consider.

Don't stop to inquire: Is this what the magazines recommend? Or will this be better than the neighbors? A better test is: Do I honestly like it? You will find yourself learning more new things, be more open to new impressions and be independently creative if you use your own abilities—honestly, truthfully, analytically.

CHAPTER XXVI

SEASONAL CHANGES

Climate dictates decoration—where the seasons give us a succession of climates, it seems reasonable to plan the colors and arrangement of a room so flexibly that we may have a summery room in summer, and yet convey in winter the sense of sheltered warmth.

New colors and rearrangement are the means of effecting such changes. It is a welcome change to introduce a new harmony of colors through the fabrics that make the slip-covers for summer use. In fact the entire color scheme may be reversed or planned in a different direction without altering the basic colors of walls and wood. Textures will carry this even farther. Rooms whose permanent or winter dress is fundamentally warm should be treated with cool, recessive tones and smooth textures.

Consider a room with neutral walls, such as off-white, brown carpet, with upholstery in browns, coppery or rust tones and yellows. For summer find blues, yellows, yellow-greens, and grays that harmonize with floor and walls; the textures should be smooth and cool-appearing, such as linen and cotton or cellophane mixtures. Prints having patterns suggesting the out-of-doors or unexciting abstractions, are good, but should not be used in such profusion as to make the whole agitated or restless. Replace heavy draperies with hangings of light airy material, hung very simply and planned to allow the entire window to be exposed at times.

Slip covers have progressed far from the old sack-like shrouds reserved for use during the family's summer absence. Today they are active, smartly tailored and tastefully planned as to color and texture. Indeed, some decorators plan chairs with two sets of slip covers, often fitted over an undercovering of only muslin or flannel. This practice permits not only quick changes of color and style for moods or seasons, but insures unintermittent cleanliness. The design and making of good slip covers is really a job for a professional upholsterer; in cities where good stores offer this service reasonably it is better economy than to attempt home-tailoring.

Furniture groupings may be rearranged with a new viewpoint toward such features as windows and doors to terraces. Fireplace groupings will be entirely subordinated, while most emphasis can be thrown upon groups or parts of the room not emphasized in winter. A room with an important window and fireplace may stress the latter in winter and the window in summer, by regrouping chairs and tables with relation to these features.

Having modified the color and texture of the important pieces of furniture, the summery picture may be heightened by bringing in small painted iron tables, plants, and accessories to replace the more substantial ones of the winter arrangement.

The small expense of summer floorings, such as grass or rush carpetings, or matting, will justify itself in added comfort and cleanliness.

BIBLIOGRAPHY

GENERAL SURVEY

Aronson, Joseph. *The Encyclopedia of Furniture*. 1938.
Bajot, E. *Encyclopedie Du Meuble*. 1900.
Clifford, C. R. *Period Furnishings*. 1914.
Eberlein, H. D., and McClure, A. *The Practical Book of Period Furniture*. 1914.
Foley, Edwin. *The Book of Decorative Furniture, Its Form, Colour and History*. 1912.
Hunter, George Leland. *Decorative Furniture*. 1923.
Johnson and Sironen. *Manual of the Furniture Arts and Crafts.* 1928.
Mumford, Lewis. *Sticks and Stones*. 1924.
Price, C. Matlack. *The Practical Book of Architecture*. 1916.
Salomonsky, V. C. *Masterpieces of Furniture Design*. 1931.
Schmitz, Hermann. *The Encyclopedia of Furniture*. 1926.
Storey, Walter Rendell. *Period Influence in Interior Decoration*. 1937.
United States Department of Commerce. *Furniture, Its Selection and Use*. 1931.

INTERIOR DECORATION

Holloway, E. S. *The Practical Book of Learning Decoration and Furniture*. 1926
——— *The Practical Book of Furnishing the Small House and Apartment*. 1922.
Jakway, Bernard C. *Principles of Interior Decoration*. 1922.
Koues, Helen. *How to Become Your Own Decorator*. 1926.
Lockwood, Sarah M. *Decoration, Past, Present and Future*. 1934.
Maas, Carl. *Common Sense in Home Decoration*. 1938.
Parsons, Frank Alvah. *Interior Decoration*. 1925.
Stewart, Ross and Gerald, John. *Home Decoration*. 1935.
Whiton, Sherrill. *Elements of Interior Decoration*. 1937.

ANCIENT FURNITURE

Richter, G. M. A. *Ancient Furniture* (Greek, Etruscan, Roman). 1926.

ITALIAN, SPANISH, FRENCH AND GERMAN FURNITURE

Byne, Arthur. *Spanish Interiors and Furniture*. 1921.
Dilke, Emilia. *French Furniture and Decoration in the 18th Century*. 1901.
Dumonthier, Ernest. *French Garde Meuble*. 1922.
Eberlein, H. D., and Ramsdell, R. W. *The Practical Book of Italian, Spanish and Portuguese Furniture*. 1915.

Felice, Roger de. *Old French Furniture*. 4 vols. 1922.
Helburn, William, Inc. (Publishers). *Italian Renaissance Interiors and Furniture*
Hunter, George Leland. *Italian Furniture and Interiors*. 1918.
Longnon, H., and Haurd, F. W. *French Provincial Furniture*. 1927.
Luthmer and Schmidt. *Empire-und Biedermeier-möbel*. 1922.
Odom, W. *History of Italian Furniture*. 1919.
Ricci, Seymour de. *Louis XVI Furniture*. 1913.

ENGLISH FURNITURE

Adam, R., and Adam, J. *The Works in Architecture of Robert and James Adam*. 1900.
Batsford, B. T. *The Decorative Work of Robert and James Adam*. 1773.
Bell and Hayden. *The Furniture of George Hepplewhite*. 1910.
Binstead, H. E. *English Chairs*. 1923.
Blake and Reveirs-Hopkins. *Little Books About Old Furniture*. 4 vols. 1911-13.
Brackett, O. *An Encyclopedia of English Furniture*. 1927.
Cescinsky, Herbert. *English Furniture from Gothic to Sheraton*. 1929.
——— *The Old World House, Its Furniture and Decoration*. 1924.
——— *English Furniture of the 18th Century*. 1911.
——— and Gribble, Ernest R. *Early English Furniture and Woodwork*. 1922.
Chippendale, Thomas. *The Gentleman and Cabinet Makers Director*. 1754.
Eastlake, Charles L. *Hints on Household Taste in Furniture, Upholstery, etc.* 1872.
Heaton, J. A. *Furniture and Decoration in England During the 18th Century*. 1889-92.
Hurrell, J. W. *Measured Drawings of Old Oak English Furniture*. 1902.
Jourdain, Margaret. *English Decoration and Furniture of the Early Renaissance*. 1924.
——— *English Decoration and Furniture of the Later 18th Century*. 1922.
——— *Regency Furniture*. 1934.
Lenygon, Francis. *Decoration and Furniture of English Mansions During the 17th and 18th Centuries*. 1909.
——— *Furniture in England from 1660-1760*. 1914.
Macquoid, Percy. *A History of English Furniture*. 4 vols. 1908.
——— and Edward. *The Dictionary of English Furniture*. 3 vols. 1924.

Singleton, E. *French and English Furniture.* 1904.

Strange, T. A. *English Furniture, Woodwork, and Decoration* (Detail drawings). 1903.

Symonds, R. W. *Old English Walnut and Lacquer Furniture.* 1923.

AMERICAN FURNITURE

Andrews, E. A., and F. *Shaker Furniture.* 1937.

Burroughs, Paul H. *Southern Antiques.* 1931.

Cornelius, Charles Over. *Early American Furniture.* 1926.

—— *Furniture Masterpieces of Duncan Phyfe.* 1922.

Dow, G. F. *The Arts and Crafts in New England, 1704-1775.* 1927,

Dyer, W. *Early American Craftsmen.* 1915.

Eberlein and Hubbard. *Colonial Interiors, Federal and Greek Revival.* 3rd Series.

Halsey and Cornelius. *Handbook of the American Wing of the Metropolitan Museum of Art.* 1924.

Holloway, E. S. *American Furniture and Decoration, Colonial and Federal.* 1928.

Hornor, W. M. *The Blue Book of Philadelphia Furniture, William Penn to George Washington.* 1935.

Kettell, R. H. *The Pine Furniture of Early New England.* 1929.

—— (Editor). *Early American Rooms, 1650-1858.* 1936.

Kimball, Fiske. *Domestic Architecture of the American Colonies and the Early Republic.* 1922.

Lockwood, Luke Vincent. *Colonial Furniture in America.* 1926.

Lockwood, Sarah M. *Antiques.* 1926.

Lyon, J. W. *Colonial Furniture of New England.* 1891.

Major, Howard. *Domestic Architecture of the Early American Republic; the Greek Revival.* 1926.

Millar, Donald. *Colonial Furniture.* 1925.

Miller, E. G. *American Antique Furniture.* 2 vols. 1937.

Nutting, Wallace. *Furniture of the Pilgrim Century.* 1921.

—— *Furniture Treasury.* 3 vols.

Nye, Alvan. *Colonial Furniture.* 1895.

Sale, Edith Tunis. *Colonial Interiors.* 1930.

Singleton, Esther. *Furniture of Our Forefathers.* 1901.

Ware, William R. *The Georgian Period.* 3 vols. 1923.

MODERN DECORATION

Abercrombie, P. *The Book of the Modern House.* 1939.

Aloi, R. *L'Arredamento Moderno.* 1934.

—— *L'Arredamento Moderno* (Second Series). 1939.

Chareau, Pierre. *Meubles.* 1928.

Corbusier, Le. *Toward a New Architecture.* 1931.

Dieckmann, Erich. *Möbelbau in Holz.* 1931.

Dorp, E. van. *Moderne Eenvoudige Meubels.*

Ford and Ford. *The Modern House in America.* 1940.

Frankl, Paul T. *Form and Re-Form.* 1930.

—— *Space for Living.* 1938.

Griesser, P. *Das Neue Möbel.* 1932.

Havelaar, J. *Het Moderne Meubel.* 1924.

Morrison, Hugh. *Louis Sullivan.* 1935.

Olmer, P. *Le Mobilier Français D'Aujourdhui.* 1910-1925.

Retera, W. *Het Moderne Interieur.* 1937.

Schneck. *Das Möbel Als Gebrauchsgegenstand Series.* 4 vols.

Schuster, F. *Ein Möbelbuch* (Modern Simple Furniture). 1933.

Todd, D., and Mortimer, R. *The New Interior Decoration.*

Wollin, N. A. *Modern Swedish Arts and Crafts.* 1931.

COLOR IN DECORATION

Adam, Robert, and Adam, James. *Color Schemes of Adam Ceilings.*

Boigey, M. *The Science of Colors.* 1925.

Carpenter, H. B. *Colour.* 1933.

Franklin-Ladd, C. *Colour and Colour Theories.*

Frohne, H. W., and Jackson, B. and A. F. *Color Schemes for the Home and Model Interiors.* 1919.

Gloag, John. *Colour and Comfort.* 1924.

Holme, H. M. *Colour in Interior Decoration.*

Houston, R. A. *Light and Colour.*

Jacobs, M. *The Art of Colour.* 1926.

Noel, Carrington. *Design in the Home.*

Pattmore, Derek. *Color Schemes for the Modern House.* 1928.

Taylor, E. J. *Colour Sense Training and Colour Using.*

Wilheim, Ostwald. *Colour Science.*

DETAILS OF DECORATION

Ackerman, Phyliss. *Wallpaper, Its History, Design and Use.* 1923.

Eberlein, H. D., and McClure, A. *The Practical Book of American Antiques.* 1927.

—— and Ramsdell, R. W. *The Practical Book of Chinaware.* 1925.

Godfrey, W. H. *The English Staircase.*

Hunter, George Leland. *Decorative Textiles.*

—— *The Practical Book of Tapestries.* 1925.

Lewis, C. G. *The Practical Book of Oriental Rugs.* 1925.

McClelland, Nancy. *Historic Wall Papers.* 1924.

—— *The Practical Book of Decorative Wall-Treatments.* 1926.

Shuffrey, L. A. *The English Fireplace.* 1912.

Williamson, Scott Graham. *The American Craftsman.* 1940.

Wyler, Seymour B. *The Book of Old Silver.* 1937.

INDEX

A

Aalto, Alvar, 120
Acacia, 235
Adam Brothers, 58, 141, 145 *et seq.*
Adelphi, 145
Amaranth, 78, 237
Arabesque, 23
Architectural backgrounds, 312
Armure, 252
Arrangement, 311 *et seq.*
Art Nouveau, 176
Arts-and-crafts, 154
Ash, 232
Aspen, 234
Asymmetry, rococo, 78
Aubusson, 260
Austria, 155
Avodire, 235
Avril, Etienne, 82
Axminster, 259

B

Bakelite, 246
Balance in arrangement, 314
Balustra, 235
Baroque, 25, 137
   English, 129
   Italian, 38
Bars, 345
Basswood, 233
Beauvais, 70
Bedrooms, 333 *et seq.*
Beech, 231
Belter, 169
Bergere, 74, 83
Bernini, 133
Biedermeier, 155
   in America, 168

Birch, 231
Bolection, 256
Bombe, 74
Bookcases, 316
Bossewood, 236
Boucher, 78
Boulle, 69
Boxwood, 235
Bric-a-brac, 268
Bristol candlesticks, 58
Broadloom, 260
Brocade, 251
Brocatelle, 251
Bubinga, 235
Bulbous turnings, 94
Bulfinch, Charles, 166
Bureau, 78
Burl, 192
Butternut, 233

C

Cabinet, 67
Cabriolet backs, 83
Cabrioli, 77, 132, 135, 139, 143
Caffieri, 69
Cane, 74, 80, 150, 241
Card tables, 135
Care of furniture, 307
Carpets, 260
Caryatids, 85, 87
Cassone, 24
Castors, 138
Catalonian chest, 41
Cavaliers, 162
Cedar, 239
Ceilings, 258
   English, 93
   French, 70
   Italian Renaissance, 23

Cellophane, 250
Chaise longue, 73, 83
Charles II, 95
Chestnut, 232
Chests, 93
Chicago Fair (1893), 169
Chiffonier, 79
Child's room, 325, 344
Chinese influence in Chippendale, 143
Chinese manner, French, 78
Chintz, 252
Chippendale, 58, 62, 140 *et seq.*
  · American, 163
Cipriani, 147
Classic modern, 176
Classic Revival, French, 81
Classicism,
    English, 145
    German, 155
    in America, 165 *et seq.*
Claw-and-ball, 133
Clipper ships, 168
Clocks, 58, 80, 270
Coco wood, 235
Colonial, 97, 100-103, 157 *et seq.*
Color, 189, 275 *et seq.*
Color schemes, 283, 348
Combination rooms, 224
Combining periods, 315
Commode, 79
Commonwealth, 90, 162
Composition, 314
Confessional chairs, 74
Confidantes, 143
Consulate, 85
Contemporary Design, 174 *et seq.*
Cork, 248, 262
Corner cupboard, 79
Credence-sideboard, French, 79
Credenza, 24
Cressent, 75, 77
Cretonne, 252
Crewel, 94
Cromwell, 96
Crotch, 192
Currier and Ives, 168
Curtains, 293

D

Damasks, 25, 251
David, 85
Daybeds, 133
Decorative objects, 199, 200, 263 *et seq.*
Dining rooms, 322, 340
Directoire, 52, 53, 84
Domino, 24, 70
Down, 302
Drake foot, 133
Drapery, 292 *et seq.*
Drawing rooms, 320
Dressing rooms, 334 *et seq.*
Duchess chair, 77, 148
Dutch Colonial, 102, 161
Dutch influence in America, 161
Dutch influence in England, 131

E

Early American, 97, 100-103, 157 *et seq.*
Eastlake, 153, 169
Ebeniste, 77
Ebony, 67, 151, 236
Eclecticism, 154
Egyptian influence, 84
Elizabethan, 92, 94
Elm, 232
Embroideries, 133
Empire, American, 106, 165
Empire, French, 84
Empire style in England, 150, 152
England, Gothic, 90 *et seq.*
England, Renaissance, 96
England, Romanesque, 91

F

Fabrics, 249 *et seq.*
Faience, 71
Faux Satine, 238
Federal, 158, 165 *et seq.*
Finishes (wood), 240
Finishing, 305
Fir, 239
Flemish foot, 134

Flemish weavers, 31
Flexwood, 256
Floor coverings, 259 *et seq.*
Fluorescent light, 289
Fontainebleau, 69
Formica, 246
Foyers, 318
Francis I, 32
Frankl, Paul T., 177
French, Classic Revival, 81
French, Empire, 84
French, Gothic, 31, 43, 44
French influence in America, 157
French influence in Chippendale, 143
French polish, 142
French, Provincial, 65
French, Regence, 74
French, Renaissance, 32
Frieze, 252
Fruitwood, 233
Functional, 176, 178, 182
Furniture buying, 297 *et seq.*

G

Gaboon, 236
Gambrel, 161
Game rooms, 345
Garde-robe, 92
Gateleg tables, 129
George I, 137
George III, 59
George IV, 152
Georgia, 162
Georgian, 63, 137, 157
German influence in America, 157, 162
Germany, 155
Gesso, 58
Gibbons, Grinling, 129, 132, 133
Gillow, 151
Glass, 244, 245
Gobelin, 69
Goddard, 164
Goncalo, Alves, 235
Gondola chairs, 80

Gothic,
English, 54, 90
French, 31
influence in Chippendale, 143
Italian, 22, 35
Gothic Revival,
American, 168
English, 140
Greek Revival, 167, 168
Gropius, 181
Guest rooms, 342
Gumwood, 232

H

Halfpenny, W. and J., 142
Harewood, 239
Harlequin furniture, 149
Hepplewhite, 59, 62, 147 *et seq.*
Herculaneum, 81, 145
Highboy, 157
Hoffman, Josef, 177
Holly, 235
Hope, Thomas, 152
Horsehair, 148
Hutch, 93

I

Ince and Mayhew, 142, 151
International style, 178
Italy, Gothic, 22
Italy, Renaissance, 23 *et seq.*

J

Jacobean, 55, 56, 58, 95 *et seq.*
James I, 94
Japanned furniture, 148
Joint-stools, 95
Jones, Inigo, 96
Jugendstil, 177
Juvenile furniture, 325, 326

K

Kapok, 303

Kas, 161
Kauffman, Angelica, 147
Kidney tables, 80, 150
Kitchen, 346
Koa, 235

L

Lacewood, 236
Lacquer, 78, 132, 135, 168, 240
Laminated wood, 226
Lamps, 286
Laurel wood, 236
Leather, 29, 253
Le Brun, 68
Le Corbusier, 181
Leleu, Jean Francois, 82
Library, 342
Lighting, 285 et seq., 334
Line, 189
Linenfold, 31, 55, 93
Linoleum, 248, 257, 261
Living rooms, 318
Louis XIII, 66 et seq.
Louis XIV, 68 et seq.
Louis XV, 48, 76 et seq.
Louis XVI, 45-47, 49, 81 et seq.
Love seats, 135
Lucite, 246
Lumiline, 289
Lyre, 83

M

McIntire, Samuel, 166
Macassar, 236
Machinery, 168, 169
Mahogany, 78, 137 et seq., 233
Mainwaring, Robert, 142
Malmaison, 85
Maple, 230
Marble, 262
Marie Antoinette, 82
Marquetry, 71, 87, 94
Mass, 189
Metals, 242 et seq.
Micarta, 246
Mirrors, 94, 197, 245, 257, 307

Mission, 170
Mixing Paints, 283
Modern, 174
Mohair, 252
Morris, William, 153
Mortlake, 94
Mosaics, 79
Moss, 303
Musical instruments, 270 et seq.
Myrtle, 236

N

Napoleon, 52, 84
Neo-Grecque, 168
Neutra, Richard, 121
New England, 97, 159 et seq.
Nonesuch Castle, 95
Norman, 92
Nursery, 326, 343

O

Oak, 231
Oberkampf, 88
Occult balance, 315
Oeben, 77
Olive wood, 236
Oriental carpets, 198, 259
Ormolu, 77
Ornaments, 268
Ornaments, Chinese, 98, 99

P

Padouk, 236
Paint (wall), 255, 283
Painted floors, 262
Painting, 101
Panelling, 61, 100, 103, 123
　　124, 256
Paul, Bruno, 177
Pearwood, 233
Pennsylvania, 162
Pennsylvania German, 102
Percier and Fontaine, 85
Pergolesi, 147
Philadelphia, 163
Phyfe, Duncan, 165

Pictures, 265 *et seq.*
Pie crust, 163
Pilgrim, 97
Pillement, 47
Pine, 60, 100, 239
Piqua, 236
Planning, 311 *et seq.*
Plants in decoration, 273
Plastics, 246 *et seq.*
Plexiglass, 246
Plush, 252
Plywood, 226
Pollard oak, 236
Polychrome, 24
Pompeii, 81, 145
Poplin, 252
Prima vera, 238
Protectorate, English, 96
Provincial French, 65
Puritan influence in America, 160
Purpleheart, 237

Q
Queen Anne, 58, 134 *et seq.*

R
Radios, 271, 272
Recamier, 168
Refectory, 94
Regence (French), 74
Regency, 63, 64, 152
Renaissance,
    French, 32
    Italian, 23 *et seq.*
    Spanish, 27 *et seq.*
Restoration, 96
Revivalism, 150
Riesener, Jean Henri, 82
Rococo, 143
    French, 76
    Italian, 25, 39
Roentgen, David, 82
Rosewood, 237
Rubber, 248, 303
Rugs, 198, 259 *et seq.*

Ruhlmann, 177
Rush seating, 241

S
Sandblasting wood, 241
Sapeli, 237
Satin, 253
Satinwood, 78, 145, 237
Saunier, Claude, 82
Savery, William, 163
Savonarola chair, 24
Scagliola, 139
Scale, 316
Scenic wallpaper, 103, 126, 127
Screens, 80, 272
Scribanne, 73
Sculpture, 267
Seasonal changes, 348-349
Secession, 176
Second Empire, 153
Sequoia, 238
Sevres, 70, 87
Shearer, Thomas, 151
Sheraton, 62, 64, 106, 149 *et seq.*
Sideboards, 150, 151
Silk, 24
Silver furniture, 133
Slant-front, 59
Slip covers, 348
Sofa, 74
Spain,
    Gothic, 27, 42
    Moorish, 27
    Renaissance, 27 *et seq.*
Spanish foot, 134
Spanish influence in America, 157
Spiral-turning, 129
Springs, 303
Stuart, 96
Swedish modern, 176, 178
Sycamore, 239

T
Taffeta, 253
Tamo, 238

Tapestry, 252
Tarsia, 24
Tea, 137
Teak, 238
Texture, 189
Tile, 262
Toile de Jouy, 50, 52, 88
Tudor, 92

U

Upholstery, 302
Urban, Joseph, 177

V

Vargueno, 29, 40
Veilleuse, 77
Velour, 252
Velvets, 25, 133, 252
Veneer, 226
Venetian blinds, 294, 295
Vermilion, 236
Vernis Martin, 78
Versailles, 69
Victoria, 153
Victorian, 169
Violet wood, 237
Virginia, 158, 162
Vitrine, 87

W

Wallboards, 257
Wall coverings, 255 *et seq.*
Wallpaper, 39, 71, 88, 101, 126, 127, 255
Walnut, 132, 134, 164, 169, 228
    Spanish, 29
Weaving, 94
Wedgwood, 87
Wicker, 241
Wiener Werkstatte, 177
William and Mary, 131 *et seq.*
Willow, 241
Windows, 291 *et seq.*
Windsor chairs, 161
Woods, 191-192, 225 *et seq.*
Wren, Sir Christopher, 96, 135
Wright, Frank Lloyd, 181

X

X-chair, 93

Z

Zebrawood, 238
Zucchi, Antonio, 147